# Worldviews and Religion

## Student Edition

CROSSROADS SERIES

Produced under the auspices of the
North American Division of Seventh-day Adventists
Office of Education

Published by
Pacific Press® Publishing Association
Nampa, Idaho

# Contents

# Your Religion Class

This section provides you with some general information about the CROSSROADS SERIES and your religion class.

## THE CROSSROADS SERIES

The CROSSROADS SERIES contains the religion curriculum for Seventh-day Adventist secondary schools, grades 9-12. This textbook is a part of the series.

## LOGO OF THE CROSSROADS SERIES

The logo of the CROSSROADS SERIES symbolizes the underlying theme of the series—that the Cross of Jesus Christ is at the very center of the Christian faith. God's revelation of Himself in the Cross reveals the only sacrifice for sin and the ultimate significance of life to each person and to every nation. Thus the Cross stands as the decisive moment of truth for all humankind through all ages. The logo, in symbolic form, portrays the centrality of the Cross with all paths (roads) of human experience and personal decisions leading to and from it.

## GOAL OF THE CROSSROADS SERIES

The goal of the CROSSROADS SERIES is to lead young people to the loving and redeeming God of Scripture. His self-revelation has its focus and fulfillment in the life, death, resurrection, and intercession of Jesus Christ, whose substitutionary death on the cross is the sole basis of Christian assurance. With Christ as Savior and Lord, each believer is enabled, through the Holy Spirit, to experience a life of worship, growth, and service, and to proclaim and stand ready for His return.

## UNITS OF STUDY—GRADES 11, 12

There are ten units of study that comprise the Religion curriculum for grades 11, 12. Each unit is published in a separate textbook. The units of study (textbooks) are:

> Daniel and Revelation
> Beliefs
> Friendships
> Romans
> Choices and Challenges
> Hebrews
> Marriage and Family
> **Worldviews and Religion**
> Life Philosophy and Moral Issues
> John

## VERSIONS OF THE HOLY BIBLE USED IN THE CROSSROADS SERIES

The NEW INTERNATIONAL VERSION, referred to as NIV, is used as the primary version of Scripture for the Anchor Text, scriptural references quoted in the narrative section of the lesson, and answers to Bible Search activities and Practical Application. Other versions of Scripture have also been used when the particular version enriches the meaning of a given reference.

## MEMORIZATION OF SCRIPTURE

Each lesson contains a verse labeled Anchor Text. Some or all of these verses will be assigned to memorize. The content of the references should first be understood, both as to its meaning and its application to your life.

The fear of the Lord is the beginning of wisdom,
and knowledge of the Holy One is understanding.

# Lesson 1

## What's a Worldview?

Do you have a life strategy, something like a 'game plan' for living?" I asked the young man sitting across the table from me. "Well," he said, "I simply accept the way the world is, and then I don't think about it a whole lot. My goal in life is to survive, keep out of trouble, party, and have a good time, but don't overdo it and hurt somebody." That's how Justin, a prison inmate, described his outlook on life.

"So you survive," I said. "What happens then?"

"You die," he quickly shot back.

"And after that?"

"Nothing. When you die, you die."

"You mean," I said, "there's no God, no heaven or hell?"

"Nope," he insisted. Then quickly looking away, he mumbled, "If there is, I'm in big, big trouble."

### The Need for a Worldview

Not to have a solid base, a realistic perspective about our existence not only means "big trouble" for life **after** death but for life **before** death as well. As human beings we crave to know the rhyme and reason of life. The longing to understand the meaning of life and the certainty of a life hereafter is part of our moral makeup. That's why we need a worldview.

### Defining a Worldview

The term *worldview* literally means "a way of seeing." It is like a pair of glasses through which we look at the world around us. It has reference to the basic assumptions by which we interpret all of life's experiences, giving our lives a sense of direction and purpose. A worldview is our understanding of reality—God, the universe, and ourselves— which serves as the frame of reference for all thought and action. In the book *Making Sense of Your World*, a worldview is described "as my blueprint for reality describing my understanding of the world and prescribing how I will live in it."[1]

Everyone is in the process of developing a worldview, even though we may not realize it. Some people have a well-defined one that they can articulate clearly, while others may be putting together a worldview of which they are not consciously aware. How about you? Have you given serious thought to your worldview? How much have you talked about it with your friends or parents?

### Evaluating Our Worldview

A worldview could be described as our map of reality. When we use maps, we generally trust them to be accurate; but, unfortunately, there may be times when they may be outdated or perhaps misleading. The same holds true for worldviews. If your worldview has faulty or inaccurate presuppositions—the primary elements that make up your worldview—then the way you interpret and evaluate life will be flawed. It's like traveling to some far-off destination when suddenly a road sign informs you that you're headed in the wrong direction. On life's journey you want to minimize such mistakes! It is imperative, therefore, that your worldview not be mere guesswork or simply reflect other people's opinions.

As we construct our worldview, it needs to be checked for reliability. While some may adopt a view of life because it's fashionable or easy-going, it is essential that we focus on the most important issues. Does our worldview accurately portray reality? Does it truly explain the significance of what's happening in our lives and in the world around us? Does it tell us the truth about life and the way things really are? It is imperative, therefore, that we have an ultimate standard by which we can test the accuracy of our worldview. Socrates said that

"the unexamined life is not worth living." Likewise, an unexamined worldview is not worth believing.

## The Need for Scripture

Worldviews are perspectives of life that are commonly derived from one's culture. Each culture gives the impression that its way of doing things is the right way to **behave** and that its outlook on life is the right way to **believe**. Consequently, the worldview each culture develops is passed on from one generation to another as a social heritage. For this reason we generally reflect the worldview in which we were raised.

It is a serious mistake, however, to merely accept the prevailing worldview of our society. As human beings we've been "blinded" to the real truth about ourselves and the world around us (2 Corinthians 4:4). From personal observation and experience alone, we cannot know with absolute assurance who we are, where we're from, or why we

are here. This is because the knowledge gained from our senses and experiences is always sinfully biased, fragmentary, and only partially true. Obviously our greatest need is to be instructed by Someone who is above and beyond our finite limitations.

Christians believe that God has made known to us a worldview that is true and unbiased. Simply put, God's word is truth (John 17:17). Knowledge that comes through His created works is known as *general revelation* and is discerned through human **discovery**. Deeper insights about life that are revealed through His Word are known as *special revelation* and are exclusively divine **disclosure**. Through special revelation, which is the Bible, God makes known the truth about the origin of life, the cause of sin and suffering, the divine remedy for evil, as well as the grand finale of all things. The heart and soul of the Christian's worldview are the revealed truths of God's Word. "The fear of the Lord is the beginning of wisdom, and knowledge of the Holy One is understanding" (Proverbs 9:10).

### Exploring Worldviews

Since every person perceives the world differently, there are as many worldviews as there are people. Some have tried to blend all worldviews into an integrated whole that will satisfy everyone. But such a scheme is unworkable. No one can consistently believe in more than one worldview because, as we shall see, the **central premise** of each is opposed by the others. At the core of every worldview is what it says about ultimate reality—who or what is "at the bottom" of everything that exists.

The practical significance of this is illustrated by a youth pastor who was talking to a classroom of school children. At the close of his presentation, he asked the children to raise their hands if they were willing to follow and obey God. All the children eagerly raised their hands except one boy. When the

**Since every person perceives the world differently, there are as many worldviews as there are people.**

pastor looked at him, the youngster quickly defended himself: "I don't want to give my life to God when I don't know what He's like." A very thoughtful answer! What God is like is the most fundamental issue of life. Unless we understand what God is like, nothing else in the Bible will make much sense.

Although there are many worldviews, scholars generally agree that the various views regarding ultimate reality can be placed into three basic categories. These are as follows:

**NATURALISM:** The basic premise of *naturalism* (as a philosophy) is that there is no supernatural realm. God, heaven, good and evil angels, and miracles are all viewed as illusions, as human inventions. Naturalism sees God as nothing more than a projection of our imagination. God is simply the highest and best that we see in ourselves. The most common expression of naturalism is *atheism*. While some atheists prefer to be called *humanists,* others are lumped together with *agnostics* or *skeptics*. What's the difference, you say? The skeptic says, "I doubt there is a God"; an agnostic states, "I don't know if there is a God"; while the atheist boldly affirms, "I know God does not exist." Perhaps the most common form of naturalism today is the *secularist* who declares, "I don't care if there is a God," choosing to live as though God does not exist.

Naturalism views the material world as ultimate reality. In other words, the physical universe is all there is. It claims that there is nothing beyond what we can see, touch, or measure. Physical matter and energy are seen as the "basic stuff" from which all existence is derived. Therefore the naturalist believes that science, not Scripture, gives us the best shot at knowing "how things really are." From such a viewpoint, all miraculous events or occult phenomena are explained as merely natural occurrences.

**THEISM:** This worldview holds that there is more than the physical world—there is a personal God who created it. *Theism* maintains that there is a radical distinction between Creator and creation. That which is created is finite. It is limited by time and space and is forever dependent upon the Creator for life. On the other hand, God is infinite. He is self-existing, immutable, eternal, unlimited—a holy God who loves, sustains, and governs what He has created. Though He is *transcendent*—beyond the universe—He is nevertheless *immanent*—active within the universe.

The theistic worldview is held by Judaism and Christianity, as well as Islam. However, while these three world religions are all *Theo-centric* (**God-centered**), only Christianity is *Christo-centric* (**Christ-centered**). *Christian theism* stands apart from Judaism and Islam in its belief that the Bible **alone** is the infallible word of God, that the God who created the world is a **Triune** God, and that Jesus Christ is the **only** means of salvation.

The Bible is the spiritual foundation of Christian theism, and at its core are three fundamental truths:

•**A personal Creator exists.** As the infinite Creator, God is the Ultimate Reality from which all other realities have their origin.

•**Created life has meaning.** As the product of an intelligent Designer, all creation has a divine purpose. As the handiwork of God, the cosmos is open to our investigation, understanding, and appreciation. As an open system, the cosmos allows for communication from God to us, as well as prayer—a person-to-person return call to the Creator.

•**God reveals His purposes.** Aware of our sin and finite limitations, God does not leave us to grope in darkness. Through His Word, He enlightens and expands our perception about Himself, the purpose of our lives, and the significance of His creation.

**PANTHEISM:** *Pantheism* (*pan* means "all"; *theos* means "god") declares that there is only one level of reality, the realm of the spiritual or the divine. The idea that all things are a unified whole, that everything exists from the same stuff, and that there is no distinction between Creator and creation is based on an Eastern philosophy called *monism*—that all is one. If all is one, then all is God; thus there is no essential difference between God, a human being, a cow, a carrot, or a rock. As a result, everything has the potential of being worshiped, as it is in Hinduism.

**We Rise No Higher
Than the God We Worship**

Pantheism sees all things as a manifestation of a divine essence. All objects are simply different forms of the same reality. In other words, something that is non-god simply does not exist. Anything that appears to be merely human is viewed as an illusion. In pantheism God is an impersonal life force, a divine essence or consciousness that energizes the cosmos. God is not "out there," but rather, He is "right here," equally within everything that exists. The New Age movement, a very popular form of pantheism in the Western world, also holds such views.

The three major concepts of God could be summarized as follows:

| Naturalism | Theism | Pantheism |
| --- | --- | --- |
| Physical Matter | Personal Creator | Divine Essence |

**OTHER WORLDVIEWS:** Though these three worldviews are the most predominant ones, there are others that are relatively significant. A worldview that lies between naturalism and theism is *deism*. Deism claims that God is entirely beyond our world, not within it. It believes that God made the world to be governed by natural laws that will ensure its orderly operation. For this reason deism rejects any kind of divine intervention, such as miracles or prayer, in the affairs of mankind. It upholds the view that God reveals Himself only through His creation; thus Scripture is seen as a human invention. Human beings are viewed as being entirely dependent upon human reason to discover within the natural world what they need to know about life.

A worldview that is between theism and pantheism is *polytheism* (also known as *neopaganism*). Polytheism reflects a radically pluralistic worldview. It's a kind of "poly" thinking in which there is no single center holding things together. Polytheism teaches that there are numerous natural or spiritual forces in the world. These forces can be in the world of nature (wind, rain, fire, earthquakes) or in the world of the occult (gods, goddesses, spirits, demons).

Polytheism is a worldview that releases humankind from the moral restraints of biblical theism and promotes a plurality of values and spiritualities. It claims to help humankind keep in touch with the richness and diversity of life. It declares that truth cannot be articulated by any one religious system, symbol, or ritual; thus many gods and goddesses are worshiped. The primary focus of polytheistic worship is the performance of rituals that are designed to appease and manipulate the gods, enabling the worshipers to get what they desire. Polytheism permeates most nontheistic religions and lies at the core of all occult spirituality.

| WORLDVIEW OVERVIEW | | | | |
|---|---|---|---|---|
| **Naturalism** | **Deism** | **Theism** | **Polytheism** | **Pantheism** |
| No God | A God | One God | Many Gods | All is God |

### Conclusion

When admiring great feats of architecture, it is easy to overlook the fact that the most essential part of the structure is hidden from view. The foundation that lies beneath the surface will only make itself apparent during a violent storm or earthquake. Our worldview is very much like that. Often hidden in the deepest recesses of our hearts, it serves as a philosophical and spiritual foundation for our lives. Eventually the rugged tests of time will reveal whether we have built on shifting sands of human wisdom or are firmly grounded on the solid Rock, Jesus Christ.

### Anchor Text

"Since the creation of the world God's invisible qualities—his eternal power and divine nature—have been clearly seen, being understood from what has been made, so that men are without excuse" (Romans 1:20).

# Reaction

## Discussion Questions

1. Why is our view of God so important?

2. Why does the average person give so little thought to his or her worldview?

3. Why is it important to see God as a person rather than an impersonal life force?

4. How can you determine the accuracy of your worldview?

5. What is the most important characteristic of God for you? Why?

6. Naturalism and pantheism appear to be opposite belief systems, yet in some ways they are very much alike. Explain.

7. What valuable truths or insights do you find in deism?

8. How is one spiritually handicapped who rejects the idea of a supernatural realm?

## Personal Response

Since the truth about God and His purpose for your life is gained primarily through the Bible, what are you willing to do to continually update your understanding of His Word?

**NOTES**

1. W. Gary Phillips and William E. Brown, *Making Sense of Your World* (Chicago, Ill.: Moody Bible Institute, 1991), p. 29.

**WRITER ACKNOWLEDGMENT OF RESOURCES**

Geisler, Norman L., and William Watkins. *Perspectives: Understanding and Evaluating Today's World Views*. San Bernardino, Calif.: Here's Life Publishers, 1984.

Phillips, Gary W., and William E. Brown. *Making Sense of Your World*. Chicago, Ill.: Moody Press, 1991.

## Bible Search

Complete the worksheet "God Reveals Himself" that will be provided by your teacher.

## Practical Application

1. Review the definitions and illustrations given in this lesson regarding a worldview. Then write six or seven sentences summarizing the key issues of a worldview.

2. Divide into groups of three or four students and read 1 Corinthians 13:9-12. Discuss the following questions:

A. What do you think Paul means by "childish ways"? How does a person put away "childish" concepts of God?

B. How have your worldviews changed since you were a child? How have your views about God changed? Explain what brought about these changes.

3. What kinds of worldviews (or view of God) are generally presented in the media—especially television sitcoms, popular movies, books, and musical lyrics? Bring to class documented evidence of a worldview presented in one of these areas that is or is not in harmony with biblical theism. Explain to the class your evidence and its probable impact on the reader or listener.

4. Draw, sketch, or cut out a picture, figure, symbol, or an emblem that represents each of the three major worldviews.

We are all pilgrims on the same journey—but some pilgrims have better road maps.

# Lesson 2

## Worldviews Make a Difference

> *Two roads diverged in a wood, and I—*
> *I took the one less traveled by,*
> *And that has made all the difference.*[1]

In 1915 Robert Frost wrote about country roads that merely diverged, and you could simply take "the one less traveled." But we no longer have such luxury! Today we find ourselves on crowded multilane freeways, where scores of highway signs inform us of changing speed limits, upcoming exits, possible detours, and which highway lane to take in order to get to where we want to go.

Driving on the interstate is a good illustration of your spiritual journey. Worldviews are very much like highway exits, each one providing you with different things to see, enjoy, and experience, but most important, each having a different destination. No doubt about it. The worldview you choose for yourself will certainly make "all the difference"!

### WORLDVIEWS AND ORIGINS

Your worldview, especially your concept of God, has a direct bearing on all your beliefs, your attitude, and your conduct. For that reason it is important that your childhood ideas of God change and mature as you grow up. The little boy who repeatedly asked his father, "Which cloud is God in?" may not reflect what you once believed. But as you continue your study of the Bible, one day you will discover that the picture of "God" you once held as a child or a teenager has dramatically changed.

### Naturalism

"Where did we come from?" is the usual starting point for all spiritual convictions. The three primary worldviews have totally different explanations for the origin of things—and thus very different life perspectives. Naturalism works from a **human-centered** position. Its basic assumption is *evolution*, that all life is the result of natural processes and that humans are merely highly evolved animals. But more important, it places humankind at the top of the pecking order, in charge of all other life forms.

Naturalism declares that the cosmos is self-existent, thus constituting ultimate reality. It maintains that the cosmos is all that is, ever was, or ever will be. One evolutionist hinted of the chance appearance of the cosmos by depicting it as simply one of those things that happen from time to time. Supposedly, through an undirected, unsupervised, and unpredictable evolutionary process, life just happened to appear on an unplanned planet adrift in space.

**Without a transcendent God, it's up to us to find the answers to questions about our origin, purpose, and ultimate fate.**

In naturalism the cosmos is viewed as a closed, self-regulating system with nothing beyond its borders. All explanations of the nature of things are accounted for within the cosmos. Without a transcendent God, it's up to us to find the answers to questions about our origin, purpose, and ultimate fate. Naturalism is very adamant about death—it is real and it represents the end of life's journey. But if we came from nothing and return to nothing, how are we supposed to find meaning and significance for our lives? One person's cynical response was: "Life is nothing more than a bus ride to the ceme-

tery, with everyone fighting for the best seats."

### Pantheism

Pantheism has at its core a **nature-centered** premise. Its basic assumption is *emanation*, a concept that all life forms are simply an expansion of a divine essence—an impersonal life force. All the characteristics of divinity are equally manifest throughout the cosmos. In other words, all living things are viewed as divine; thus nothing dies but simply reincarnates. Reincarnation differs from a bodily resurrection in that a person can reincarnate into any animate or inanimate object.

A pantheistic view of the origin of life has in recent years become very popular. This is especially true for those in the Western world who see the inadequacy of a godless explanation, while at the same time, do not want to accept the idea of a personal Creator as revealed in Scripture. Pantheism maintains that a divine consciousness permeates the evolutionary process, and this is why design and orderliness characterize the world of nature.

Pantheism views the cosmos as a closed system governed and controlled by karma—a universal law of cause and effect that determines one's fate in each lifetime. The meaning of life is to be found in creation itself. The earth, seen as a living organism and the source of all life, is to be revered and worshiped. This kind of "creation spirituality" views all living things as having equal worth and equal rights. Thus no real distinction is made between the value of a child, a dog, or a termite. Imagine the devastating impact upon society where the oneness of all things blurs the significance of diversity and uniqueness within creation.

## Theism

Christian theism is a **Creator-centered** worldview. Its basic assumption is divine *Creation*, that a Creator God brought the cosmos into being. Orderliness, intricate interdependence, and beauty in the natural world are seen as evidences of God's creative activity rather than a chance process. The creation of humankind in God's image is a key biblical concept. It reveals our capacity of having a relationship with our Creator, it provides the basis for our dignity and worth, and it spells out our unique position as the Creator's representative on the planet. Theism affirms that the distinctions and diversity one finds in the world reflect God's design. As illustrated in the following graphic, as **creatures**, people and animals are **alike** in that they are all subject to God's sovereign rulership. As **persons** created in God's image, humankind is **distinct** from the rest of creation, possessing individuality, creativity, and the power to think and

Persons [ **Creator**
**humans** ] Creatures
**animals** ]

choose. In our relationship to other creatures, humankind was to have dominion, the God-given task of being the caretaker of the environment. The position as custodian of the lower created order was patterned after God's loving rulership over all things. After the Fall, this God-given dominion was twisted into self-serving domination. Disregard of God's ultimate rulership has led humankind to either worship or exploit the world around it. Such spiritual confusion has led to either gross idolatry (Romans 1:25) or to massive destruction of God's creation (Romans 8:22).

The utter disparity between naturalism and Christian theism is vividly illustrated by their views of "the beginning." In naturalism, earth's muddy slime randomly spews forth the first elements of life, while in Christian theism, the earth's soil is in God's hands being lovingly shaped into human form and empowered with life. And we're still in His hands, "for in him we live and move and have our being" (Acts 17:28). Such intimate care and involvement by the Creator instills creation with supreme significance and worth. Though science can **measure** what already exists, God alone can give it value and **meaning**.

Because the Creator is benevolent and intelligent, the cosmos is good and orderly. It functions on the premise of uniformity, in harmony with the law of cause and effect. The cosmos is an open system, open to God's intervention and sustaining power. When "bad things happen to good people," however, this aspect of the theistic worldview can be difficult to accept or understand.

God's sovereignty, however, does not take away our power to choose; thus the possibility of sin, suffering, and death exists. For the Christian, death is real but not final. Death has been conquered by the Life-Giver, giving all those who believe in Him the blessed hope of life eternal at the resurrection.

| Naturalism | Theism | Pantheism |
|---|---|---|
| Evolution | Creation | Emanation |
| Human Focus | God Focus | Nature Focus |

## WORLDVIEWS AND SALVATION

Violence, pollution, sickness, and death have become the trademark of our planet. Though all acknowledge that something is seriously wrong, there is no agreement as to why human beings act the way they do and what can be done about it. In other words, each worldview offers its own perspective as to the nature of the **problem** and the needed **solution**.

### Naturalism

From its atheistic viewpoint, naturalism sees humankind as being basically **"good."** As the highest of all evolved creatures, the human dilemma is simply a matter of human **limitations**—our failure to divest ourselves of "lingering animal instincts" in our evolutionary ascent. The solution offered by naturalists is education—the intellectual development of human thought and spirit.

With no Deity to turn to, naturalism depends totally upon human resources to resolve the ills of the planet. Without a God-given premise, sin and salvation are not viewed as realities. Humankind may be weak and frail, diseased and addicted, but not sinful. They may be victims in need of support and treatment, but not rebels in need of redemption. They may be inhibited and insecure, but nothing that a large dose of self-esteem can't resolve. Naturalism sees religion as meaningless and outdated, offering people pious delusions instead of practical solutions. Further, it condemns Christianity as distracting us from earthly concerns, prohibiting us from helping ourselves, and denying us the opportunity of reaching our full potential. Paul indicted the naturalists of his day when he declared, "The man without the Spirit does not accept the things that come from the Spirit of God, for they are foolishness to him" (1 Corinthians 2:14).

### Pantheism

Since pantheism views humankind as essentially divine—as **god**—it rejects Christianity's belief that humanity is separated from God. Thus salvation from sin is unnecessary. Pantheism contends that our real problem is one of ignorance of our divinity, of our divine self. From a pantheistic perspective, it means that the solution to our problems lies within ourselves.

Much of pantheism's appeal is due to its rejection of a Creator God in favor of an inner divinity. Whereas the God of Scripture requires submission to His authority and holds out high moral expectations, pantheistic spirituality is self-defined and self-serving, catering to the ever-popular notion of unlimited human potential. An exhilarating self-centered focus is what makes the New Age movement, a pantheistic lifestyle, so attractive and appealing in today's world.

In Christianity we recognize our **lostness** apart from God; in pantheism the focus is on humankind's **oneness** with Deity. Pantheists believe that Christians are in a state of illusion, referred to as a "normal consciousness." Pantheists believe that such an illusory state can be extinguished only through *enlightenment*. Enlightenment is to experience an "*altered consciousness*" (a trance-like state), which is gained through various mind-altering techniques such as Eastern yoga, transcendental meditation, and hallucinatory drugs. The more altered

## Only in Christian theism does a transcendent God break into the cosmos to rescue a dying world.

one's state of consciousness, the closer one is to realizing oneness with the divine. To fully achieve enlightenment is known as "*god-consciousness.*"

### Theism

Several years ago a second-grade boy wrote a paper for his teacher that contained this intriguing comment: "I believe that so many twins are being born into the world because little children are afraid of being born into the world alone." He's right! This

world is indeed a frightening place, and by ourselves, we're no match for the spiritual plague that has ravaged and ruined our planet.

In contrast to the other worldviews, Christian theism depicts human nature as basically **sinful**. The Bible declares that sin is so extensive and deeply rooted in our lives that the **only** solution is redemption through Jesus Christ. In other words, the impact of sin upon God, the cosmos, and humankind is so comprehensive that only God Himself can resolve it. Only in Christian theism does a transcendent God break into the cosmos to rescue a dying world. Only the God of Scripture has wounds— "pierced for our transgressions . . . crushed for our iniquities," for "by his wounds we are healed" (Isaiah 53:5).

From the biblical viewpoint, sin needs to be understood from two perspectives. First, sin describes our **nature**, our natural **condition**. Entering this world apart from a relationship with the Creator, our hearts— the control centers of our lives—are naturally self-serving and rebellious. Unless corrected, this sinful bias leads us to remain independent of God, or as the Bible says, "Each of us has turned to his own way" (Isaiah 53:6). In essence, sin is rejecting God's rightful place in our lives and placing self on center stage.

Second, **sin** has reference to the **effects** of evil, our moral **conduct**. This would include everything we say and do that is not in harmony with the laws of God. Sin's deadly impact creates an addiction for evil and blinds us to reality—our lost and dying

*The Good News is not good news to those who believe that they are already good.*

condition (Jeremiah 17:9). Our alienation from God negatively affects all our relationships—with ourselves, with others, and with the rest of creation.

But Christianity meets the challenge with an all-encompassing solution: Whatever sin **ruins**, salvation **restores**. Separation of God and man is dealt with in the person of Jesus, who united in Himself both God and man. When we are "in Christ," by virtue of our faith in this unique God-man, the penalty for our rebellion against God is forgiven, our relationship with Him is restored, and our natures are re-created and empowered by the Holy Spirit, giving newness of life to all our relationships.

| Naturalism | Theism | Pantheism |
|---|---|---|
| Sin is: *Human Limitations* | Sin is: *Spiritual Separation* | Sin is: *Human Ignorance* |

## WORLDVIEWS AND ETHICS

### Naturalism

How one views the beginning of human existence determines how one interprets the **past**, lives in the **present**, and prepares for the **future**. All of these are largely decided by one's choice of an ultimate frame of reference. In naturalism self usurps that position; everything centers around "me." In an attempt to live without God, the naturalist has no divine reference point to gauge his or her thoughts and actions. Without an eternal perspective, moral values are entirely relative to one's own needs and experience. There are no absolutes, no objective standard of right and wrong. Any kind of moral judgment becomes a matter of preference rather than principle. When one believes in humankind's natural goodness, "good" is whatever a person deems best at the moment. In such an arrangement, self-interest becomes the overriding motive. In naturalism, each person is ruler of his or her own realm.

### Pantheism

Obviously, pantheism's claim that everything is of one essence has a very definite effect on one's ethical beliefs and behavior. Claiming equality with deity, the pantheist simply turns inward in search for an ultimate authority. Upholding the oneness of all things, pantheists view reality as transcending any and all distinctions, including good and evil. Believing that all reality is divine, pantheists conclude that evil is merely an illusion.

The pantheistic worldview that evil does not exist encourages its followers to become involved with the supernatural realm without fear of a demonic reality. For this reason, religions steeped in pantheism, such as Hinduism in India or New Age in the United States, not only foster immoral behavior but swing open the door to occult experiences and demon possession.

### Theism

In Christian theism God is the central point, the absolute standard, by which all moral judgments are based. Eternal principles of right and wrong reflect the very nature of God; thus all human behavior is to be measured against that yardstick. We are generally unaware, however, of the degree of selfishness that is at the root of all our thoughts and actions. In order to discern the subtle and pervasive nature of sin, we need the spotlight of God's Word to bring to our attention the real extent of self-serving. That's one reason why people don't like to read the Bible. It's so much easier to conform to the world's standards and simply do what seems right or feels good. God intends that the Scripture convicts us of our sin and safeguards us from the heart's natural tendency toward self-centeredness and idolatry.

## CONCLUSION

In each worldview one's understanding of the problem determines the choice of a solution. If we do not correctly discern the chief cause of our ills, how can we hope to correct them? Only when sin is acknowledged as the underlying problem does Christ's gift of salvation have any significance. In other words, only where sin is recognized is a Savior needed.

Christianity stands alone in its offer of a living Savior to a dying world. While other religions still await a Messiah, pay their respects to dead prophets, or bow to images of gods and goddesses, Christianity points to an uplifted cross and an empty tomb. The fact that we worship a Savior who lived, died, and arose again for our salvation is what ultimately **makes all the difference!**

## Anchor Text

"Although they knew God, they neither glorified him as God nor gave thanks to him, but their thinking became futile and their foolish hearts were darkened. Although they claimed to be wise, they became fools and exchanged the glory of the immortal God for images made to look like mortal man and birds and animals and reptiles. . . . They exchanged the truth of God for a lie, and worshiped and served created things rather than the Creator—who is forever praised. Amen" (Romans 1:21-25).

21

**NOTES**

1. Robert Frost, "The Road Not Taken," 1915.

### Bible Search

1. In its estrangement from God, humankind tends to either exploit nature or worship it. The world as a whole suffers the dire consequences of these destructive practices.

A. According to Genesis 1:26-28 and Psalm 8:1-9, how is humankind's unique value and distinctive position within creation described?

B. What does Isaiah 24:4-6a say are the reasons for humankind's assault on creation?

# Reaction

## Discussion Questions

1. What are the main reasons why people reject the existence of a personal God?

2. What is the basic difference between reincarnation and resurrection?

3. How can a person know that the Christian worldview is right?

4. What is the primary difference between Christian conversion and pantheism's enlightenment?

5. How would you answer the naturalist's argument that Christianity denies humankind from reaching their full potential?

6. How should Christians respond to the killing of animals for food, for sport, or for laboratory experiments?

7. How do you respond to the accusation that "Christian" societies are guilty of wantonly abusing and destroying nature?

## Personal Response

As you compare Christian theism with other worldviews, what spiritual blessings do you now more fully recognize and appreciate? Your lesson states that "whatever sin ruins, salvation restores." What has sin ruined in your life that you want Christ to restore for you?

2. In naturalism and pantheism the inner spirit (nature) is viewed as naturally good; in Christian theism it is seen as basically sinful. When the naturalist and the pantheist look within, they believe they are looking at the **solution**. On the other hand, the Christian theist views the inner man as the **problem**.

What does God have to say about this issue? Read the following texts and write how each one specifically describes the condition of the human heart.
A. Psalm 51:5-10
B. Jeremiah 17:9, 10
C. Mark 7:20-23
D. Romans 1:20, 21
E. Romans 7:18, 19

## Practical Application

1. Write a skit or organize a panel in which three people, each one representing a different worldview, discuss this question: Why do bad things happen to good people?

2. Pair up with another student, discuss the following question, and share your conclusions with the class: In what ways does Christian theism simplify a person's life, and how does it complicate it?

3. Your teacher will divide the class into small groups and assign each group one or more of the concepts found within the various worldviews. If you were to accept the concept(s) assigned to you as true, explain what impact it would have on your life.

People do not reject the Bible because it contradicts itself
but because it contradicts them.

# Lesson 3

## Is One God Enough?

Have you ever noticed as you walk through a city park or a school campus that no matter how many sidewalks there are, there are always enticing shortcuts—narrow, well-beaten paths across lawns and through flowerbeds, back alleys, and even ditches? As president of Columbia University, David D. Eisenhower came up with a system that effectively solved this problem. He observed where students walked across the campus and then simply paved the pathways they had made for themselves. However, such a practical solution for laying sidewalks doesn't work for religion. Jesus warned us about merely following the paths where the majority has walked.

Religion is not something that is followed just by good people; it is universally practiced. Biblical and secular records make it clear that there was never a time when religion did not exist. Spirituality is deeply rooted in human nature, but this does not imply that everyone has a saving knowledge of God. It means that each of us has a sense that life is not just an accident, that there's more to life than what we can see. We all have a deep longing for that which goes beyond ourselves, an inner void that can be satisfied only by God Himself.

### COMMON CHARACTERISTICS OF RELIGION

It has been said that the world doesn't need a **definition** of religion as much as it needs a **demonstration**. As true as that may be, it is important that we understand what is meant by *religion.* First, religion focuses on a core of established beliefs and practices generally derived from sacred writings and cultural traditions. These core beliefs may relate to issues of ultimate concern or moral principles that govern everyday life. Second, religion usually embraces the worship of a higher power and allegiance to an ultimate authority. Finally, religion involves personal devotion as well as corporate observance of religious customs and festivals.

Religions generally have universal as well as cultural (local) characteristics. Universal characteristics are those held in common with other belief systems, whereas cultural ones are distinctive beliefs that set a religion apart from the others. The attempt to blend the beliefs of various religions is called *syncretism,* while the effort to emphasize the unique aspects of a religion is called *fundamentalism.* Syncretists build **bridges** to promote unity between religions while the fundamentalists erect **boundaries** to protect their beliefs from other religions. World religions, Christian denominations, and even local churches (including Seventh-day Adventists) may at times be sharply divided between emphasizing common ground or upholding distinctive beliefs. Both can serve a useful purpose, however, when viewed as complementary perspectives.

### Worldviews and Religion

Religions are generally an outgrowth of worldviews. The following chart lists some of the religions and philosophies that flow out of the major worldviews.

| Naturalism | Theism | Pantheism |
| --- | --- | --- |
| Buddhism | Judaism | Animism |
| Confucianism | Christianity | Hinduism |
| Humanism | Islam | Taoism |
| Marxism | | New Age |

While these world religions offer great diversity as to belief, practice, and lifestyle, their followers tend to share common desires and concerns. In ever-increasing numbers, believers of various religions have crossed geographical and cultural boundaries to live and work together. In some cases they may be next-door neighbors and best friends. Thus there's a great need for sympathetic understanding and awareness of the basic needs of all people regardless of their religion, such as the eradication of disease, famine, human suffering, and war, as well as the protection of human rights and the environment.

### Evaluation Is Imperative

In our world the impact of good and evil is evident in every area of life, including religion. History vividly shows that religion can be redemptive and useful but also very cruel and destructive. Abuses and oppressive practices carried out in the name of religion can be open and obvious or at times very deceptive and insidious. The Bible warns us that "Satan himself masquerades as an angel of light" (2 Corinthians 11:14). "It is not surprising, then, if his servants masquerade as servants of righteousness" (verse 15). Evil is best disguised when it intermingles truth with falsehood and hides its real intentions with apparent goodness.

It is imperative, therefore, that every religious experience, belief, or practice be carefully appraised. "Do not believe every spirit, but test the spirits to see whether they are from God" (1 John 4:1). As Christian believers, it is our responsibility to identify and defend that which is true and expose that which is false and misleading.

## THE UNIQUENESS OF CHRISTIANITY

Christianity embraces three fundamental principles that clearly set it apart from all other world religions. These three principles are:

- **Only one (triune) God exists.**
- **The Bible is God's only infallible revelation.**
- **Jesus is the only mediator to God.**

This lesson deals with principles one and two; principle three is covered in the next lesson.

### 1. Only One God

The issue of who and what God is lies at the heart of all religions. And as we have learned, each worldview has a concept of God that is utterly different from the others.

Yet most world religions (except theistic religions) believe that all people worship a common god. It is maintained, even by some Christians, that each religion simply identifies this universal "god" by a different name. But that's only half true. Created gods do **receive** their names from their makers, names that express **human** qualities. This is a common heathen practice. The uncreated God, however, has chosen to **reveal** His name to us, for He alone is qualified to disclose His **divine** attributes.

The significance of a name is clearly illustrated by how quickly certain emotions or memories are stirred up when someone's name is mentioned. For example, every time I hear the name Weaver, a childhood next-door neighbor family, I think of their daughter, Bazooba Jane. I can still feel the shock and dismay I felt when I heard her name for the first time. It's almost as bad as the first daughter of the Biddle family. When she was born, her parents couldn't agree on a first name, and so they decided to name her Friday February Eleven Biddle. Perhaps these two girls might be some of the 60,000 people in the United States who each year change an undesirable name.

In the Bible, names played a very important role; thus they were not flippantly chosen. Knowing another's name was a special privilege that signified openness and friendship. In revealing His name(s), God demonstrated His desire to be known and understood by His people. As a name distinguishes one person from another, so God's name is designed to set Him apart from false gods. A name signified a person's character. A "good name" referred to one's reputation, and for that reason God was very protective of His names. Some of the severest threats in the Bible were pronounced against those who profaned or blasphemed the name of God. Such an act was seen as an unwarranted attack on God's holy character. God declares, "I am the Lord; that is my name! I will not give my glory to another or my praise to idols" (Isaiah 42:8).

"I am the Lord . . . ; apart from me there is no God" (Isaiah 45:5) is a dominant theme of the Bible. In fact, many see the Old Testament as "a battle of the gods." In ancient times victorious nations saw their victory as a triumph of their gods. The liberation of the Jewish people was a humiliating defeat of "the gods of Egypt" (Exodus 12:12) and an obvious demonstration of the supremacy of Israel's God. The plagues were designed to show the uselessness of the Egyptian deities and to provide an opportunity for the Egyptians to turn to Israel's God. In all the conflicts between Israel and their enemies, God's power and prestige was on the line. Vindi-

## He is not the God of any one nation, culture, race, or religion.

cation of God has always been a key issue in the warfare between good and evil, and especially so at the end of time, when the world will once again experience the plagues (Revelation 16).

Another important aspect in Israel's struggle with the surrounding nations was to make known that God was not simply one of many tribal gods. He was to be acknowledged as the "Lord of all the earth" (Joshua 3:13). He is not the God of any one nation, culture, race, or religion. He is God "of all the nations," and "all the ends of the earth" are to recognize this fact (Isaiah 52:10). As the Creator, His sovereign rule has no boundaries and acknowledges no limitations.

### 2. Only One Infallible Revelation

Christian theism affirms the Bible as the ultimate standard, enabling us to be impartial in discerning good from evil. It views the Bible as the divine measurement by which everything else is judged. Church

creeds and pronouncements, religious traditions, and our personal reasoning and feelings are all subordinate to God's revelation. This does not mean, however, that our reasoning powers are to be ignored. Both divine revelation and human reason (spiritual reflection) are essential in the Christian life. For example, one legitimate function of our reasoning ability is to interpret and apply God's revelation. But if human reason is given priority, it is easy for us to rationalize and use our powers to explain and justify things in a self-serving way. Our reasoning powers can be trusted only if they are submissive to God's Word, for our thoughts are not His thoughts (Isaiah 55:8).

Since all major religions have sacred writings, the question naturally arises as to why Christians claim that only the Bible is the true word of God. Why can't the Bible be seen as simply one of many equally inspired writings? Such a position is untenable, however, because the writings viewed as sacred by the other world religions, as you will discover, present **opposing** viewpoints on all **underlying** issues. This is attested by the fact that the worldviews of non-Christian religions, derived from their religious writings, stand in stark contrast to the teachings of the Bible. Thus one could logically conclude that either all "sacred" writings are false or that perhaps one is genuinely true.

In support of the premise that the Bible is the only authentic revelation, Christians point to the following data:

First, Jesus accepted the Bible of His day (the Old Testament) as the authentic Word of God. He declared it to be "the truth" (John 17:17), thus approving its teachings on the nature of God, the creation of human beings, and the reality of sin and salvation. In all of these key issues the entire Bible stands in agreement, but in direct opposition to what is taught in the "sacred" writings of other religions. For the Christian, Christ's affirmation of the Old Testament authenticates the Bible, and the Bible only, as the infallible Word of God.

Second, Christianity is a historical religion, meaning that its fundamental teachings are integrally linked to historical events. For example, the gift of salvation is based on the reality of a historical event— the life, death, and resurrection of Jesus. Thus the truths of the Bible can either be affirmed or denied, depending on whether the historical event can be validated. On

# The truths of the Bible can either be affirmed or denied, depending on whether the historical event can be validated.

this point, noted archaeologist Nelson Glueck declares, "It may be stated categorically that no archaeological discovery has ever controverted a biblical reference."[1]

The impact of this is illustrated by the story of a third-grade teacher who pointed to a city on her desk globe and asked, "How do we know that such a city exists if we've never been there ourselves?" After a few moments a girl raised her hand and said, "If I turn the globe to the place where I live and I see it is right about that, then I can know that the globe is right about all the other places." Likewise, verification of historical events in Scripture has, in effect, validated the truthfulness of all its claims.

## The Sin of Idolatry

Idolatry is holding a view of God that is not in harmony with God's revelation of Himself in the Bible. In our sinfulness we instinctively conjure up notions about God that are false and misleading. What makes matters even worse is that we are generally unaware of our idolatry. In several surveys, when Christian teenagers were questioned about their obedience to the Ten Commandments, the one commandment that was always singled out as the one they felt was the easiest to keep was the commandment regarding the worship of idols. The truth is that idolatry is the **root** of all other sins, the infinite God being replaced by earthly things. Idolatry is exalting anything **created** higher than the **Creator**. This is the basic premise of the worship of gods and goddesses of ancient civilizations, as well as today's heathen cultures and world religions.

The Creator made humans in His own image, but sin has twisted this around; thus we attempt to conform God to our likeness (see Psalm 50:21). It's like stuffing God into the container of human thoughts and desires. Thus the trademark of idolatry has always been the making of gods that have human traits and characteristics. The gods of the Greeks and Romans, for example, fought, cheated, hated, and loved just like humans. That the God of Christianity is so unlike sinful humanity is evidence that He is obviously not the product of human imagination. People desire a deity who meets their self-serving needs; thus they have a natural hostility to a god who is holy, unchanging, self-existing, and sovereign.

Heathen nations made idols to represent the gods they worshiped. They imagined for themselves "user-friendly" gods who made no moral demands. However, the gods needed to be powerful enough to deliver whatever the worshiper wanted: victories at war, good crops, and large families. By the use of magic, incantations, and rituals,

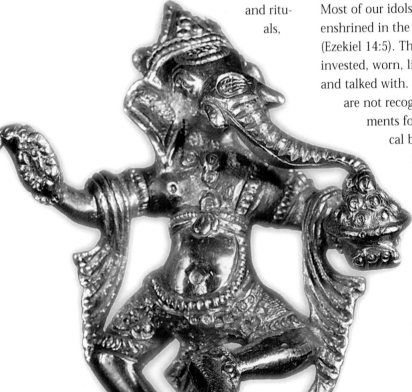

they asked their gods to control nature, to fulfill dreams, and to assuage fears. Things haven't changed much. These are still the promises of neopaganism today.

**The Subtlety of Idolatry**

The danger of idolatry is just as real for Christians as for nonbelievers. "My dear friends, flee from idolatry" was Paul's warning to Christians of his day (1 Corinthians 10:14). This implies that idolatry remains a threat even though we know that idols are false and unreal. Keep in mind that everything around us is a potential idol. Naiveté about idolatry is like the mistake made by the city of Troy as its people gladly welcomed the Trojan horse (filled with enemy soldiers) into their city. The Bible makes clear that idolatry is not simply bowing down to crude objects of wood or stone. Most of our idols are invisible, secretly enshrined in the throne room of our hearts (Ezekiel 14:5). They can be bought, parked, invested, worn, lived in, or perhaps walked and talked with. Generally speaking, they are not recognized as obvious replacements for God. For example, physical beauty, intellectual attainments, and personal accomplishments are often idolized, receiving greater adoration than God Himself. How often do we see sports heroes, movie stars, political figures, or entertainers the object of passionate devotion? More

30

than likely, idols will come in the form of simple attractions that wedge themselves between us and God. Paul makes this point clear by associating idolatry with selfish ambition, human greed, sexual impurity, jealousy, and coveting (Galatians 5:20, 21; Ephesians 5:5). In other words, an idol is whatever occupies center stage of your life.

In summary, idolatry is pinning our hopes and dreams on a lie. Idols misrepresent God and lead us to self-serving illusions of grandeur, power, and control. They seductively deceive us into thinking that we can win the world and save our souls at the same time. That's the oldest sin around! Idolatry involves wrapping our lives around a substitute for God, because only with a substitute can we remain the ruling center of our lives. The world's need is not for a plethora of gods that make all kinds of alluring promises, that only disappoint and enslave. **One God is enough**, if He is the One who came and died on Calvary's cross, thus confirming the truthfulness of all the other promises He has made to us.

## Anchor Text

"There is one body and one Spirit—just as you were called to one hope when you were called—one Lord, one faith, one baptism; one God and Father of all, who is over all and through all and in all" (Ephesians 4:4-6).

### NOTES

Nelson Glueck, *Rivers in the Desert: A History of the Negev* (New York, N.Y.: Farrar, Stauss & Cudahy, 1959), p. 31.

 **Bible Search**

1. The lesson states that God's names serve a very important role in that they distinguish Him from all other so-called gods. Read the following texts that deal with the names of God and write out what important truth about God is taught in each text.
   A. Exodus 3:13, 14.
   B. Leviticus 19:12.
   C. 2 Chronicles 7:14.
   D. Psalm 8:1.
   E. Psalm 124:8.
   F. Acts 4:12.
   G. Philippians 2:5-9.
   H. Revelation 14:1.

2. A dominant theme of the Bible is the supremacy of God and the fallacy of idols. Read the following texts and write what God says about His superiority to man-made idols.
   A. Deuteronomy 4:32-39
   B. Isaiah 41:21-24.
   C. Isaiah 43:10-12.
   D. Isaiah 45:5, 6.

3. The Bible clearly states that we are not to judge others (Matthew 7:1, 2) or to judge from outward appearances (John 7:24). On the other hand, the need to judge religious beliefs and practices is not only permissible but essential. According to the following texts, write out what the appropriate response of believers would be as they encounter other belief systems.
   A. Isaiah 8: 19, 20.
   B. 1 Thessalonians 5:19-22.
   C. Hebrews 4:12.
   D. 1 John 4:1-4.

# Reaction

1. When you hear the word *religion,* what first comes to your mind? Explain why.

2. Why is it important for a Christian to believe that the Bible is the only infallible revelation of God?

3. What evidence is there that supports the idea that every person is religious or spiritual by nature?

4. How can you know whether there are "other gods" in your life? How do you determine when something has reached the "god" status in your life?

5. Do you know the meaning of your first or last name? Find out and share it with the class. Explain what significance, if any, its meaning has to you.

6. It has been said that the extent to which you misunderstand the character of God, to that extent you worship an idol. What are some misunderstandings of God you have recently heard or held yourself?

7. Many believe that the thousands of gods of all the world's religions are really the same "God"—just with different names? Do you agree or disagree? Explain your answer.

8. What biblical stories can you think of that clearly demonstrate the power of God over man-made gods?

## Personal Response

What are your most prized possessions? Who are the people who mean the most to you? What is it that receives your highest admiration or your utmost attention? In light of these questions, what significant changes would you be willing to make so that God is truly God in your life?

## Practical Application

1. The lesson states that within every religion (and church), there are two significant perspectives—building bridges and erecting boundaries. Divide into groups of three or four students and discuss these issues as they relate to the Seventh-day Adventist Church. Use the following ideas as guidelines for your discussion and be prepared to share your conclusion with the class:

   A. In what ways are both of these perspectives essential to the life and ministry of the church?

   B. What are the dangers in carrying out these objectives?

   C. Which of the two seems to be emphasized more than the other today? Explain why you think this is so.

   D. Suggest some Bible texts that support or serve as guidelines for these two perspectives.

2. You have just read a letter published in the editorial section of your newspaper, which states that the key to world unity and peace is recognition by the peoples of the world that all worship the same God. Write a one-page letter of rebuttal.

3. Select a song or make a collage that identifies or glorifies the "gods" of today or illustrates their impact and power on people's lives.

Christ is the Light, which lights every person that comes into the world.

# Lesson 4

## Only Two Altars

*Absolute Confusion!* The title of the book immediately caught my attention. I wondered what the book was all about. Gang violence in Los Angeles? Big city traffic? Some ugly disasters that have become so commonplace? As I scanned the front cover of the book, I was startled by the answer to my question. The book was about "lifestyles, trends, habits, and religious views in America."[1] From his extensive surveys, the author concludes that though Americans generally have a wide exposure to many different religions, they have a very superficial understanding as to what they're all about. They mistakenly assume that all religions teach the same things and worship the same God, so why bother to study them? Granted, religions are alike in many ways; nevertheless, it is crucial that we understand their differences and why divergence came about.

### From One to Two Altars

After Adam and Eve yielded to Satan's temptations, God dealt with their nakedness by slaying an animal, which provided coats of skins for them to wear. By this highly symbolic and heart-wrenching sacrifice, God revealed His decision not to simply **condemn** sinners or **condone** sin but to personally **atone** for what had been done. Rather than require the guilty to die, God chose an innocent substitute to die in their place. In so doing, both the gravity of sin and God's mercy were clearly demonstrated. Since "it is the blood [death] that makes atonement" for sin (Leviticus 17:11), God, through Jesus Christ, symbolically offered Himself as a sacrifice to die in the sinner's behalf. From that day forward, the first family gathered around one common altar and in faith offered their sacrifices to the Lord.

The first biblical account of any significant change in the worship of God is the story of Cain and Abel and the two altars on which they placed their offerings. In God's **acceptance** of Abel's slain lamb and His **rejection** of Cain's garden produce, the principles of true and false religion are clearly demonstrated. Just as God had earlier disapproved of Adam and Eve's attempt to cover their nakedness with sewn fig leaves, He now rejects Cain's efforts to gain divine favor by the work of his own hands. In these simple stories, the ABCs of salvation are plainly taught: Relying on human **attainment** identifies false religion, and trusting in divine **atonement** characterizes true religion.

Since the time of Cain and Abel, many new "altars" have been erected, each one holding a different sacrifice, each one representing a different way to God. But lest we become confused or overwhelmed with the abundance of choices, there's a simple principle to keep in mind. From a biblical perspective, there are **only two altars**—for there are only two kinds of religion. There is human-centered religion—God favorably responding to what **people are doing for themselves**, and God-centered religion—people favorably responding to what **God has already done for them**. The truth is that every person eventually chooses to worship before an altar that represents either God's way or the human way of salvation. The Bible knows of no other options.

### Confronted by Many Gods

During the early stages of their history, the Jews faced scores of deities and religions of local tribes and ancient civilizations. From 600 to 200 B.C., they were surrounded by an explosion of major religions: Confucianism, Taoism, Buddhism, Shintoism, and Zoroastrianism. (Some of these will be studied in a later lesson.) Most of these religions, with their pagan philosophies and idolatrous practices, were a continual challenge to the theistic beliefs of the Jewish nation.

In this "contest of the gods," God made it known to His people that they were not to serve or bow down to any foreign gods. The issue was very simple: If you were not worshiping and serving the **true** God, then you were worshiping and serving a **false** one. The "god" of other religions was an **idol**, viewed as an **enemy** (Psalm 96:5). The incident of Daniel's three companions being cast into the fiery furnace for refusing to worship the "golden image" is an illustration of the intense confrontations experienced by God's people through the cen-

turies. While the Jews were inhabitants of their own land, God gave specific commands to utterly destroy the heathen people with their idolatrous religions and pagan gods. God also declared that anyone within the Jewish nation who "sacrifices to any god other than the Lord must be destroyed" (Exodus 22:20). On the positive side, the Jews were to make known to "all the peoples of the earth" the one and only true God. He was to be exalted as the "God of gods and Lord of lords" (Deuteronomy 10:17), and all who came to Him were to approach, worship, and serve Him on His own terms.

When Michelangelo was asked what method he used for sculpting his statue of David, he replied, "It's quite simple. You just take a chunk of marble and chop away everything that doesn't look like David." Perhaps this illustrates how Christianity related to Judaism. Christianity took from Judaism the idea that there is only one God and only one true religion. Then it chopped away everything that didn't look like Jesus. In Christianity, Jesus is clearly displayed as the unique Son of God, the ultimate revelation of God, and the only basis of salvation. The New Testament does not view Christ as one Savior among many. He is proclaimed **the** Creator of all things, **the** only Mediator between God and humankind, **the** Redeemer without whom all will perish, **the** One who comes as King and Judge to decide the final destiny of all nations.

### The Only Way

As stated in the previous lesson, the third fundamental principle that sets Christianity apart from all other religions is that Jesus is the only way to God. Jesus expressed it this way, "I am the way and the truth and the life. No one comes to the Father except though me" (John 14:6). "I am the gate; whoever enters through me will be saved" (John 10:9). Not only are Christ's words clear and unequivocal, they fully agree with the underlying theme of Scripture that salvation is not **achieved** by human effort but **received** through Christ by faith. The righteousness that saves is never our own; it is the righteousness of Another, namely, Jesus Christ, our Substitute. But human nature basks in its own goodness, prides itself in its accomplishments, and extols its own worthiness. Thus any teaching that rejects people's best efforts in saving themselves is very offensive to many of the world religions. What Paul declared 2,000 years ago is still true, "The message of the cross is foolishness to those who are perishing, but to us who are being saved it is the power of God" (1 Corinthians 1:18).

Christianity's high and lofty claims for Jesus are not well received by today's world religions. Let us examine four common ways that people respond to this Christian belief.

### Exclusivism

*Exclusivism* refers to Christianity's claim that **only** the followers of Christ worship the one true God and that salvation comes **only** through faith in Jesus Christ. In other words, "My religion is not only true, it is the only truth." Exclusivists point out that the Scripture **never** states that salvation is received from idols, pagan gods, or heathen

religions. In fact, God consistently warns of the extreme dangers and utter worthlessness of heathen gods and characterizes them as "abominable idols" and "a snare" to His people (Jeremiah 32:34; Judges 2:3). Nevertheless, those religions that make exclusive claims for their particular view of salvation, such as Judaism, Christianity, and Islam, are often compared very negatively with so-called tolerant religions like Hinduism, Taoism, and Buddhism.

### Inclusivism

*Inclusivism* **broadens** the claims of exclusivism by saying that while Christianity may be uniquely true and valid, salvation is accessible in other religions. It's saying: "My religion is true for me; your religion is true for you." Genuinely good people of any religion will not be excluded from salvation just because they have not subscribed to the unique claims of Christianity. While inclusivists believe that an act of faith is necessary for salvation, they contend that this faith need not be directed toward Jesus. In other words, people may be saved even if they do not know about Jesus per se. God grants them salvation if they sincerely believe in their "god" as revealed in creation, in their conscience, or in their culture.

This brings us to a decisive question: Does any religion, if sincerely believed, save the believer? Does faith save even though it may be deficient or misdirected? In answering this question, we must keep in mind that faith, like a coin, has two sides: the **act** of faith—the **process** of believing, and the **object** of our faith—the **person** in whom we believe. If we are saved simply **because** we have faith, then faith is our savior, and in whom we believe is irrelevant. On the other hand, if we are saved **through** faith, if faith is only our way of making contact with One who can save, then the One in whom we place our faith is all important. The New Testament supports the latter premise: "It is by grace you have been saved, through faith" (Ephesians 2:8). "And if Christ has not been raised, your faith is futile" (1 Corinthians 15:17). In Christianity, faith never **makes** salvation; it simply **takes** the gift offered. Faith does not bring salvation into existence; faith is believing and accepting what God has already provided for us in Jesus.

### Pluralism

*Pluralism* maintains that people can have a saving relationship with God within any world religion because all of them are **equally** viable paths to God. It's saying, "All religions are equally true." Like *universalism*, it maintains that in the end all humankind will be saved. Since all forms of knowing are relative and conditioned by time and space, it declares that no religious ideology is universal and absolute. Pluralism insists that when a religion makes absolute claims for itself, such claims lead to intolerance, hatred, and violence.

Pluralism, like multiculturalism, endorses the attitude of political correctness—the idea that one shouldn't do or say anything that another group might find offensive. Pluralism is based on relativism, which declares that all values and religions are equally valid. The goal is universal tolerance, that no one position is to be judged better than any other. To label anything as bad is wrong; to see everything as good is right. For the pluralist, tolerance is of paramount importance.

Pluralism's relativistic attitude forbids anyone from judging a religion as true or false, or labeling a religious belief good or evil. The only thing bad is intolerance, thus promoting the dangerous idea that people can never be wrong about what they believe. Pluralists would not want us to distinguish between a religion whose symbol is a degrading idol and a religion whose symbol is an uplifted cross. What about such practices as the Inquisition, Crusades, human sacrifices, caste system, female infanticide, widow burning, satanic worship, the castration of young boys to retain their soprano voices for church choirs—all done in the name of religion? If pluralism is correct, it would be impossible to discriminate between a Mother Teresa and a David Koresh.

### Atheism

In contrast to pluralism, which accepts all religion as valid and good, atheism rejects all religion as illusory and false. While in pluralism it is impossible for religion to be wrong, in atheism it is impossible for religion to be right. Simply put, "All religions are untrue; none of them will save you." In order for atheism to be correct, it must demonstrate that religions at all times and places have been destructive illusions. It allows for no positive contributions. On the other hand, if pluralism is correct, it must verify the fact that all religions are basically good and equally valid. It must substantiate

## Four Views About Salvation

| Exclusivism | Inclusivism | Pluralism | Atheism |
|---|---|---|---|
| Saved only through Christ | Saved through any religion | Everyone will be saved | Religion never saved anyone |

its claim that all religious pathways lead to God, leaving no possibility that some may lead to death, hell, and destruction. As Christians, we should avoid the undue negativism of atheism and the unrealistic optimism of pluralism.

### What Does It All Mean?

First, no matter what our views may be regarding the world's religions, it must not diminish our recognition of God's universal love for all humankind and that all of His acts are consistently gracious, fair, and just. In Revelation 15:3, 4, the redeemed utter these words as they sing of God's deliverance: "Great and marvelous are your deeds, Lord God Almighty. Just and true are your ways. . . . All nations will come and worship before you, for your righteous acts have been revealed." In the judgment we will be judged according to the light we have received. No matter how dim the light, those who want to see it can, and no matter how bright the light, those who do not want to see, never will.

Second, the Bible spells out very clearly that we are "Christ's ambassadors" to a lost and dying world (2 Corinthians 5:20). This means that we are to preach the gospel "in all the world for a witness unto all nations" (Matthew 24:14, KJV) and "make disciples of all nations" (Matthew 28:19). One of the final commands of Scripture is to "proclaim to those who live on the earth—to every nation, tribe, language and people" the eternal truths of salvation (Revelation 14:6). If salvation is already found in every religious pathway and belief system, then the directive to preach the gospel—the good news of **God's** salvation—has no meaning or purpose. Christians must reject any view that minimizes or ignores the biblical mandate to take the gospel to nonbelievers.

Third, seeing ourselves as a chosen people has many pitfalls. The Israelite nation was chosen by God to be a witness to the Gentiles, but this special privilege was eventually undermined by an attitude of superiority and elitism. Christians can also be tempted into thinking that their proclamation of the exclusive claims of Jesus gives them an exclusive status.

Finally, tolerance can be a very convenient virtue in a world where diversity is the norm. G. K. Chesterton once remarked that tolerance is the virtue of a man without convictions. Putting it in another way, tolerance can easily be used as an excuse for failing to witness, refusing to become involved when evil is being done, or giving in to error rather than speaking up for the truth.

On the other hand, rightfully used, tolerance can be a means to a good end. It can be used as a tool to preserve the **liberty** of all religions, though not necessarily their **equality**. As surely as we must safeguard the rights of individuals to hold to ideas different from our own, we must also protect the rights of people to express their convictions or to challenge the beliefs of others. The recognition of error is perhaps the most important step toward human understanding and wisdom. In today's world, it is imperative that diversity be respected, that tolerance be practiced, but above all, that truth be cultivated and cherished.

 Anchor Text

"Even if there are so-called gods, whether in heaven or on earth (as indeed there are many 'gods' and many 'lords'), yet for us there is but one God, the Father, from whom all things came and for whom we live; and there is but one Lord, Jesus Christ, through whom all things came and through whom we live" (1 Corinthians 8:5, 6).

### NOTES

1. George Barna, *Absolute Confusion!* (Ventura, Calif.: Regal Books, 1993).

### WRITER ACKNOWLEDGMENT OF RESOURCES

Clendenin, Daniel B. *Many Gods, Many Lords.* Grand Rapids, Mich.: Baker Books, 1995.

Gaede, S. D., *When Tolerance Is No Virtue.* Downers Grove, Ill.: InterVarsity Press, 1993.

Sanders, John, editor, *What About Those Who Have Never Heard?* Downers Grove, Ill.: InterVarsity Press, 1995.

 **Bible Search**

1. Complete the worksheet "Bridging the

40

# Reaction

## Discussion Questions

1. How do you respond to the concept that a person is either saved or lost, that there is no third option?

2. What is the rationale for God's command not only to destroy heathen idols but to destroy the idol worshipers as well?

3. Why does God not allow sinful people to atone for their sin by accepting their best efforts to do good?

4. How can Christians practice tolerance, yet at the same time stand up boldly for their faith and beliefs?

5. How would you answer the claim that God is too loving and merciful to destroy those who have not responded favorably to the truths of Christianity? In what way does Christ's death on the cross reveal the very definite limitations of tolerance?

## Personal Response

Are you willing to lift up Jesus as the only way of salvation in a world where the popular thing is to view all religions as equally valid? Are you willing to not use tolerance as an excuse for not witnessing to those whose views are different from your own?

Great Divide" that will be provided by your teacher.

2. Divide into groups of three or four and discuss the following question: How much merit does inclusivism have? Is it a biblical teaching? Read the following texts regarding the salvation of the heathen and write a summary paragraph that reflects the conclusion of the entire group. Texts: Isaiah 45:22; Isaiah 49:6; John 1:9; John 3:18, 19; Romans 1:20-23; Romans 2:11-16.

3. In Acts 17:16-31 there is a clear presentation of New Testament teaching regarding idolatry. Read this passage of Scripture and answer the following questions:

   A. What is Paul's attitude toward idolatry? Does it differ from that which is depicted in the Old Testament? (verse 16).

   B. List six characteristics of God in the Scriptures that set Him apart from the gods of the Greeks (verses 24-29).

   C. What statement does Paul make in verse 30 regarding all forms of modern idolatry in today's society and heathen religions?

   D. According to verse 31, by whom and on what authority will the world be judged?

## Practical Application

1. The Cain and Abel story is a very perceptive account of the different religious experiences of two young men. Either rewrite this story in a modern setting, contrasting the spiritual perspectives of two Adventist teenagers that illustrate the principles brought out in the lesson or draw a picture of two altars on which there are objects that illustrate the two kinds of religion.

2. Divide the class into groups and have them take opposing sides to debate the following statement: The attempt to persuade others to change their religion because we think they are mistaken is being judgmental and is therefore wrong.

3. Write a skit illustrating how a Christian can effectively share his or her belief that Jesus is the only way to God while at the same time showing tolerance to the other person who believes that a mediator is unnecessary. Before writing the skit, read John 4:7-26 for some very clear insights regarding this issue. Be prepared to present the skit to the class.

4. In 1990 a book titled *What Do We Mean When We Say God?* was compiled by Deidre Sullivan and published by Doubleday. In conversation with hundreds of people of different ages, backgrounds, and religions, she asked them this very provocative yet fundamental question about God. Interview at least ten people in your family, school, church, or neighborhood and ask them the same question. Write out the responses you receive and conclude your paper with a paragraph describing what you learned from doing this project.

Choice :.. not chance, is what determines destiny.

# Lesson 5

# The Great Controversy

Thornton Wilder, in *Our Town*, gives the following address to one of the characters mentioned in the play:

> **"Jane Crofut**
> **The Crofut Farms**
> **Grover's Corners**
> **Sutton County**
> **New Hampshire**
> **United States of America**
> **Continent of North America**
> **Western Hemisphere**
> **The Earth**
> **The Solar System**
> **The Universe**
> **The Mind of God"**[1]

Not only are each of us personally etched in the mind of God, He is the Ultimate Center of all reality. Only as we come to know Him and His Word can we rightly interpret the significance of everything else. This holds true whether we're dealing with the reality of goodness and truth or the existence of sin and conflict. Our world has endured the most hideous kinds of strife, revolutions, and world wars, but only in Scripture are we made aware of the warfare that underlies all other conflicts—*the great controversy*. While its breadth encompasses the universe, its depth reaches the innermost recesses of our hearts. There are no exemptions in this war; everyone is a participant in this life-and-death struggle, whether we like it or not.

The **"great controversy"** motif is the comprehensive framework through which most Christians, especially Seventh-day Adventists, view and understand the entire span of human history. According to this paradigm, the attention of the entire universe is focused on an unrelenting conflict between the forces of good and evil, both seen and unseen, that began before humankind was even created.

## The Divine Government

The primary focus of the great controversy is Lucifer's attack on Heaven's rulership and authority. Since the character of

God is the very foundation of the divine government, it is obvious that the focal point of the initial rebellion was God Himself. God knew that He could not defeat Lucifer by merely displaying superior strength but only by demonstrating the depths of His love and the rightness of His laws. The following graphic serves as a symbol of God—the great **"I AM"**—the eternal, self-existent One.

God is the ultimate wellspring of **life** and of **love**, as well as the universal administrator of **law** and justice. These unique attributes are the very heart of His nature and character, and they serve as the infrastructure of His government. In God's plan for the universe, created beings were designed to live within loving relationships. The Creator's love for them was to serve as the model for all other relationships. This divine pattern would not only keep intact the union between God and created beings, it would also ensure peace and harmony throughout the universe. For this to happen, all creatures were to depend upon their Creator for guidance as to how life was to be lived. They needed to understand that the outworking of love was to be safeguarded by a moral framework of divine law that was to be freely chosen and obeyed by all.

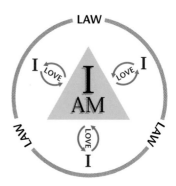

There is a delicate and essential relationship that exists between law and love. As illustrated above, the **principles** of divine love are found within the **parameters** of God's law. It is God's Word that gives love its content and direction, that provides a flawless explanation of how "real love" works. In other words, love's role is to **inspire**, to motivate us to obey God and serve others, whereas the role of law is to **instruct**, to define what obedience to God and serving others really means. Love and law are complementary, each playing an important role in maintaining order and stability, while upholding the spirit of unselfishness.

## Lucifer Challenges God

Lucifer was the first to seriously question God's authority and rulership. During the initial stages of his protest, Lucifer claimed he was not in rebellion against God but that he merely wanted to improve the divine government. Viewing God's laws as "an unnecessary restraint,"[2] he promoted the idea of unrestricted freedom. Lucifer clamored for a higher level of existence—one of absolute freedom—a life without divine

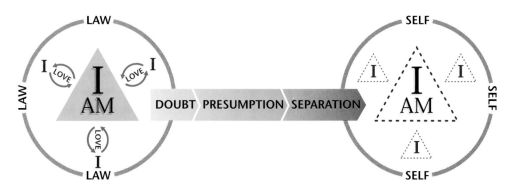

restrictions. He reasoned that holy, sinless beings were capable, in and of themselves, of making the right choices. Driven by the desire for Godlike autonomy, Lucifer eventually boasted, "I will sit enthroned. . . . I will make myself like the Most High" (Isaiah 14:13, 14).

## A Rival System Established

There were three basic steps Lucifer took in establishing a rival kingdom. The first step was **doubt**. He **challenged reality** as it then existed, questioning the fairness of God's government and the necessity of moral laws. The second step was **presumption**. He **created an alternative**, assuming that his self-seeking proposals would improve God's government. The final step was **independence**. He **chose separation**, declaring his independence from God's sovereign rulership and establishing a self-centered existence. This led to a "war in heaven" (Revelation 12:7), resulting in Lucifer (now called Satan—the adversary) and the angels who sided with him to be expelled (verse 4). Their relationship with God was forever severed as the focus of their loyalty switched from God to themselves (see 2 Peter 2:4). In Satan's choice to become his own god and establish a rival kingdom, sin emerged as an ugly reality within a once holy universe. In *Paradise Lost* Milton writes of Lucifer's hellish scheme in these words: "To reign is worth ambition, though in hell. Better to reign in hell, than to serve in heaven."[3]

## Rebellion Kindled on Planet Earth

After Satan was cast out of heaven, a strategy session was held with those who had joined him in opposing God. Here plans were laid to tempt earth's newly created inhabitants into taking the same three steps Lucifer had taken in his rebellion against God—thus Satan's three beguiling statements spoken to Eve in Eden (Genesis 3:1-5). If Adam and Eve could be enticed to follow in Satan's footsteps, this planet had the potential of becoming the primary arena from where the rebels could continue to promote their revolutionary ideas. It was their hope that the revolt would prove so appealing that it would spread throughout God's vast domain. When Adam and Eve yielded to temptation and planted the banner of rebellion on this planet, our world did indeed become "the lesson book of the universe."[4] However, the exact opposite of what Satan hoped for took place. Sin's utter failure, climaxing in the death of Jesus, serves as a guarantee that sin will never arise again—anywhere in the universe.

Perhaps the best summary as to why Adam and Eve yielded to Satan's temptations is expressed in this statement: "It was distrust of God's goodness, disbelief of His word, and rejection of His authority, that made our first parents transgressors, and that brought into the world a knowledge of evil."[5] From their personal experience of shame and guilt, of pain and grief, they learned firsthand the awfulness of sin. It was God's plan that humankind's knowledge of sin be gained through divine **revelation**, never by human **participation**.

### The Consequences of Sin

The ultimate tragedy of Adam and Eve's choice was that it brought the entire human race into Satan's rival kingdom. With humanity's source polluted by sin, all members of the human family are born separated from God and sinful in nature (Psalms 51:5; 58:3). We are born "I" centered, for "self-seeking" is the "very principle of Satan's kingdom."[6] We enter this world with an inbred tendency toward evil and a resistance to that which is holy. Being born in the kingdom where self reigns, we are naturally fearful of God and opposed to His laws that are to govern our lives. "The sinful nature desires what is contrary to the Spirit. . . . [For] they are in conflict with each other" (Galatians 5:17).

Each of us is born on a battlefield, **personally** involved in an on-going struggle between finding security in God's wisdom and strength or allowing unbelief, pride, and self-sufficiency to be our guiding principles. The whole course of human history is primarily a record of each succeeding kingdom building its own Tower of Babel. From the stone age to the space age, from ancient Babel to spiritual Babylon, all people, in heart, are builders of Babylon—a biblical symbol of our **defiance** of God's rulership and our **reliance** upon human resources.

### The Human Dilemma

Since each person is born a rebel, independent of God and out of harmony with the principles of heaven, how can we personally be held accountable for something that was not of our choosing? It's not our fault that we're born into a world that is at war with God, where every person is infected with a self-serving spirit, where each stands condemned before God for being antagonistic to His rulership. How can God save us from such a dilemma, while at the same time show Himself fair and just in light of these accusations? In John 3 Jesus gives us a straightforward answer: "God did not send His Son into the world to condemn the world, but that the world through Him might be saved. He who believes in Him is not condemned; but he who does not believe is condemned already, because he has not believed in the name of the only begotten Son of God. And this is the condemnation, that the light has come into the world, and men loved darkness rather than light" (verses 17-19, NKJV).

### God's Solution to Our Sinfulness

In the above verses, Jesus points out that humankind is not condemned for being **born** sinful but for refusing to **believe** what God has done about our sinfulness. In other words, we are not condemned for **arriving** in a sin-darkened world but for **remaining** in darkness after being enlightened to God's redemptive plan through Jesus Christ. Though it was Adam's choice that separated humankind from God, it is our choice to accept or reject God's offer of reconciliation with Him.

To have our relationship with God restored means that our citizenship has to be transferred from the kingdom of darkness to the kingdom of light; it means that our allegiance has to be switched from the creature to the Creator; it means we must be set free from being slaves to this present world—**doomed to die**, and be adopted into God's inner circle—**destined to live**.

And how is such an exodus from Satan's kingdom to God's kingdom to be accomplished? In the same way Israel experienced their Exodus from Egyptian slavery. As the lamb's blood on the doorposts saved the lives of believers and sparked their exit from Egypt, so our only hope of deliverance from the dominion of sin is through "the Lamb of God"—Jesus Christ. Salvation is our **exodus** from an unbelieving world under Satan's control and our **entrance** into the fellowship of believers under the Lordship of Jesus Christ. "He [God] has delivered us from the dominion of darkness and transferred us to the kingdom of his beloved Son, in whom we have redemption, the forgiveness of sins" (Colossians 1:13, 14, RSV).

### The First and Second Adam

A central theme of the New Testament is the concept of *corporate oneness*, that all of humanity is linked together in a common life and a shared identity.[7] Corporate oneness implies that when Adam fell into the pit of sin, the whole human race fell with him. Since humankind is simply Adam's life multiplied, the result (not the guilt) of Adam's sin has been passed on to us—separation from God, a sinful nature, and condemnation by the law for our sinful condition. If the negative side of corporate oneness is that we all fell in the one man, Adam, the positive side is that God likewise redeemed us all in the one man, Jesus Christ, the "second Adam" (Romans 5:12-21). The history of these two men—Adam and Christ—has affected the eternal destiny of all humankind. Scripture declares that "in Adam all die" and that "in Christ all will be

## Jesus Christ became the substitute and representative of the human family.

made alive" (1 Corinthians 15:22). Simply stated, "in Christ" we pass from eternal death to eternal life (John 5:24).

Through the miracle of the Incarnation, Jesus Christ united in Himself our humanity with His divinity. Through this mysterious union, Christ qualified to become the second or "last Adam" (1 Corinthians 15:45). In the Hebrew language, *Adam* means "mankind," and as the second Adam, Jesus Christ became the substitute and representative of the human family. In Him every requirement of salvation has been fulfilled in our behalf. In Him reconciliation between God and humankind has been accomplished through His life, death, and resurrection. When Jesus died as our Savior on the cross, every human being died on the cross "in Him." As Paul declares, "I have been put to death with Christ on his cross, so that it is no longer I who live, but it is Christ who lives in me" (Galatians 2:19, 20, TEV). In Christ we paid the penalty for sin required by God's broken law and were delivered from the condemnation that was ours in Adam. Thus Paul can boldly exclaim, "Therefore, there is now no condemnation for those who are in Christ Jesus" (Romans 8:1). In Christ we are not only restored to God's **favor**—justification, we enter into the process of being restored to God's **likeness**—sanctification. As our faith lays hold of the gift of salvation, the Holy Spirit initiates within us a new life of spiritual growth and obedience to God. In salvation, faith is not a **substitute** for obedience, but rather,

baptized into his death? . . . If we have been united with him like this in his death, we will certainly also be united with him in his resurrection" (Romans 6:3-5). In other words, the holy history of Christ becomes the history of the believer because he is in Christ by faith. Only by being identified with Christ's **history** can we have a share in Christ's **future**!

### The Other Worldviews

In biblical times Israel was viewed as being at the "crossroads" of the world. Two of the

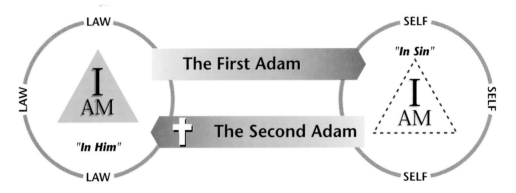

the **stimulant** for all true obedience.

But like any gift, God's offer of salvation has to be accepted in order to be experienced and enjoyed. When a person accepts the gospel and is united by faith to Christ, immediately all that Christ has provided as humankind's substitute is made effective for that person. All that Jesus accomplished while on this earth—His oneness with the Father, His perfect obedience to God's law, and His death on the cross—is imputed (credited) to the believer through faith. Paul puts it this way: "Don't you know that all of us who were baptized into Christ Jesus were

world's greatest civilizations surrounded Israel, and they eventually became Israel's primary enemies. Egypt to the south enslaved Israel for over 200 years while Babylon to the north held them in captivity for 70 years. These two great kingdoms defiantly opposed Israel's God and scorned His messengers, as the ten plagues and the fiery furnace so dramatically demonstrated. Today Christianity is on a similar collision course with two worldwide spiritual foes—naturalism and pantheism. Though the confrontation is different, the conflict is just as real. Naturalism and pantheism can just as surely destroy God's people today as Egypt and Babylon conquered their rivals in biblical times.

Within these two worldviews—and all the religions that flow out from them—there is no great controversy motif, since both worldviews hold to the idea that there is only **one** basic reality. Falsehood and deception are their most powerful weapons! Naturalism declares that only the natural or physical world exists. Consequently, there is no place for a spiritual controversy between the forces of good and evil. On the flip side, pantheism maintains that there is only a spiritual or a divine realm; thus the two opposing kingdoms are **merged** into one reality where no evil exists.

In any conflict the objective of the enemy is to camouflage its whereabouts and to give misleading signals as to its intentions. In the great controversy, Satan gains a tremendous advantage when his existence is distorted or denied, for then unwary people are easily caught off guard and ensnared by his sophistry and deceptions. It is imperative, therefore, that we understand for ourselves the truth about our enemy in God's Word. Only in the Scripture is the reality of Satan clearly established, his methods of attack openly exposed, and the means by which he can be overcome plainly revealed. No wonder Satan tempts us to crowd out of our lives meaningful Bible study. He knows that it's our most powerful weapon against him.

Today's musical lyrics, movies, television, and news media are just some of the avenues that glorify and popularize naturalistic or pantheistic ways of thinking and living. As you sense the forces of good and evil

waging an all-out war in your own heart and soul, fortify your mind daily with what God says in His Word. Being fed by God's Word and focusing on God's Son is Heaven's prescription for victorious living!

## Anchor Text

"This controversy between God and the dragon began years ago in heaven. God's Son Michael and the loyal angels fought against the dragon and his angels. . . . The great dragon that was defeated and cast out of heaven with his angels was Satan, that ancient serpent also called the devil. He and his angels were hurled to the earth and are trying to deceive the whole world" (Revelation 12:7-9, The Clear Word).

**NOTES**

1. Erdman Harris, *God's Image and Man's Imagination* (New York, N.Y.: Charles Scribner's Sons, 1959), pp. 17, 18.

2. Ellen G. White, *The Great Controversy* (Nampa, Idaho: Pacific Press, 1950), p. 495.

3. Michael S. Horton, ed., *Power Religion* (Chicago, Ill.: Moody Press, 1992), p. 28.

4. Ellen G. White, *The Desire of Ages* (Nampa, Idaho: Pacific Press, 1940), p. 19.

5. Ellen G. White, *Education* (Nampa, Idaho: Pacific Press, 1952), p. 25.

6. Ellen G. White, *The Desire of Ages* (Nampa, Idaho: Pacific Press, 1940), p. 436.

7. Jack Sequeira, *Beyond Belief* (Nampa, Idaho: Pacific Press, 1993).

## Bible Search

1. God's law was not only the key issue in the great controversy; it remains a divi-

sive issue in Christendom today. Ever since Lucifer planted the seeds of rebellion, the divine law has been maligned, misunderstood, and misused. Thus Paul's admonition, "We know that the law is good if one uses it lawfully" (1 Timothy 1:8, NKJV), is still very applicable for our day. In this assignment you are going to discover the proper function and use of God's law. Read the following texts and then write a 150-word summary describing the appropriate and inappropriate responses to God's moral law. TEXTS: Romans 3:19, 20, 28, 31; Romans 5:20; Romans 7:7-14, 22-25; Romans 10:1-4; Galatians 2:16; Galatians 3:24; 1 John 5:2, 3.

2. We need to understand that the **universal** dimension of the great controversy is not simply a Seventh-day Adventist belief

# Reaction

### Discussion Questions

1. What do you think are Satan's ultimate objectives in his continuing rebellion against God?

2. Why did God allow Satan to come to this planet and tempt Adam and Eve?

3. Why do people generally attempt to gain acceptance with God and eternal life through good works rather than by faith?

4. Do you think Satan visits other inhabited worlds and actively promotes his revolutionary ideas? (see Revelation 20:1-3).

5. Can you give some examples from the Bible that illustrate the truth of corporate oneness?

6. How does your understanding of the great controversy affect your attitude toward God?

7. Why is the death of Christ sufficient ground to argue that sin will never rise again, anywhere in the universe?

but an underlying theme of Scripture. Read the following texts and then write a 150-word summary describing how these details of the great controversy affect your view of God, sin, and salvation. TEXTS: Revelation 12:7-12; Job 1:6, 7; John 8:44; John 12:30-32; 1 Corinthians 4:9; Ephesians 6:12.

3. The great controversy also has a **personal** dimension—a spiritual warfare within the heart—that each of us experiences every day of our lives.

A. How is this inner conflict described by Paul in Galatians 5:17? See also 2 Peter 1:3, 4.

B. What does each side produce when it gains the upper hand? (Galatians 5:19-23).

C. What brings victory to the Christian in this warfare? (Galatians 5:24).

## Personal Response

Do you have any misgivings about how God related to Lucifer's rebellion and the fall of our planet? Are you willing to write out questions about the great controversy that really bother or perplex you and bring them before the Lord in prayer, asking Him for wisdom and understanding?

## Practical Application

1. Prepare a two- or three-minute devotional in which you share a personal experience, or that of someone else, in which a real spiritual battle was fought and how victory was gained.

2. Choose one or more of the visual graphics in your lesson and draw one that is different from those in the lesson, but which accurately portrays a particular aspect of the lesson.

3. Your lesson states that people will be condemned in the judgment for choosing to remain separated from God and clinging to what this world has to offer, even though they have been enlightened by the gospel. Make a collage, find a song, or write a short story that illustrates why people choose the amenities of the world rather than God's gracious offer of salvation. Or interview ten people, asking them the same question and writing their responses and your personal conclusions in your report.

Preach the gospel at all times. . . . If necessary, use words.

# Lesson 6

## Our Christian Roots

"My ancestors came over on the *Mayflower*!" Maria shouted across the classroom as we talked about family trees. It was obvious that some of the students were skeptical, but her intensity and excitement suggested that she was telling the truth. Just as Maria found out, exploring your roots can bring all kinds of new insights and meaning to your family's past. The Christian Church is very much like a family, with roots that go back nearly 2,000 years. Just as a family enlarges and subdivides into distinct family units, Christianity has also changed, grown, and experienced many divisions since its beginning.

### Facts About Christianity

Christianity is the world's largest religion, comprising nearly 30 percent of the world's people. Of the 1.6 billion Christians, 63 percent are Roman Catholics, 28 percent are Protestants, and 9 percent are Eastern Orthodox. These statistics vary greatly with each nation. For example, in the United States, 75 percent of Christians are Protestant, 22 percent are Roman Catholic, and 3 percent are Eastern Orthodox.

The birthday of the Christian Church is generally seen as occurring at Pentecost, when the first believers were energized by a mighty outpouring of God's Spirit. The nucleus of this new religion was people who believed that Jesus was the promised Messiah of the Old Testament and accepted Him as their Savior and Lord. For several decades Christianity was not seen as a world religion, but simply as an "offshoot" of Judaism. The fact that the followers of Jesus first worshiped on Sabbath in synagogues encouraged such a notion. Believers also held worship services in their homes since no thought was given to building churches because of their belief that Christ would return in their lifetime.

Luke declares in Acts 11:26 that "the disciples were first called Christians at Antioch." This nickname, originating sometime during the first century, was not chosen by the believers themselves. It was probably a derisive term coined by the pagans to ridicule the people whose beliefs and lifestyle were so different from the general population. The term *Christian* appears only three times in the New Testament, its last usage being Peter's admonition, "If you suffer as a Christian, do not be ashamed, but praise God that you bear that name" (1 Peter 4:16).

### Christianity Grows Up

The primary thrust of the first believers was their commitment to and their proclamation of a profoundly simple message—Jesus Christ had died for the sins of the world and was resurrected on the third day as foretold by Scripture (1 Corinthians 15:3, 4). Paul stated it succinctly when he wrote to the Corinthians, "I resolved to know nothing while I was with you except Jesus Christ and him crucified" (1 Corinthians 2:2). The initial trademark of Christianity was its focus on the life and sacrifice of Jesus, its acceptance of the Old Testament, and tangible evidence of the Holy Spirit in the lives of the believers.

As a baby quickly grows out of infancy and childhood and plunges into the competitive and complex world of a teenager, so Christianity rapidly entered an era challenged by religious squabbles and oppressive surroundings. During a period of nearly 250 years, spiritually divisive issues became widespread within the Christian Church, while harsh criticism and severe persecution by Roman authorities assaulted Christianity from without. Despite such extreme difficulties, Christianity continued to prosper and grow, and by the beginning of the fourth century, 25 percent of the population of the Roman Empire was Christian.

### Reasons for Christian Differences

There were several reasons why differences and disputes emerged rather quickly within Christianity. Some were due to rapid growth and expansion. Christian churches had sprung up on three different continents—Europe, Asia, and Africa—and many of these churches represented various cultures and customs, each having different needs and concerns. At the same time, Christianity was also being persecuted by a hostile pagan environment. Faced with these serious challenges, Christianity was compelled to clearly define and defend what it stood for. Since Christianity was not handed a nicely organized set of beliefs and practices, vigorous debate ensued for several centuries as to what constituted the Christian religion. Thus the early challenges experienced by Christianity were actually blessings in disguise. In the very process of searching the Scripture to resolve religious dissension, the content of the Christian faith was formulated. The challenge was compounded, however, by the fact that many believers did not have access to the writings we now call the New Testament. These twenty-seven books were not officially recognized as an authoritative *canon* until the end of the fourth century.

### Resolving Christian Controversies

During the first five centuries, several key issues generated a great deal of heated debate. The primary way that Christianity responded to major controversies was through church councils. A council was a gathering of church leaders who met to discuss and resolve the issues at hand. Through this process it was decided that Christians were not obligated to keep Jewish ceremonies as a basis of salvation, and the doctrine of the Trinity was established by affirming the equality of Jesus, the Holy Spirit, and God the Father. It was also determined that humankind was inherently evil and could not save itself by its good works.

Other issues that were dealt with were church leadership and authority, the pattern of church worship, the use of images and relics, and the question of which writings should be included in the New Testament.

By the fourth century, the verdicts handed down by church councils became known as *creeds*. These documents were so named because they all started with the word *credo*, a Latin word meaning "I believe." A positive aspect of creeds was that they brought doctrinal unity to Christianity. The negative side was that at times they reflected human reasoning more than the teachings of God's Word. Too often creeds were mistakenly seen as the final word on a particular issue, and for some, they eventually became more authoritative than the Bible. Unfortunately, such tendencies still exist. We, too, must avoid the attitude that all truth has been discovered and that all doctrines have been determined. The beliefs that have been handed down to us must be thoughtfully compared with Scripture, as well as personalized and made relevant to the times in which we live. But most important, we need to understand that the underlying purpose of all our beliefs, doctrines, and creeds is to amplify and make real the love of Jesus and His saving grace.

## Radical Changes Within Christianity

During the Middle Ages (500–1500), Christianity went through a transformation that radically altered its course. These changes were so significant and far-reaching that it resulted in two momentous events that permanently divided Christianity—*The Great Schism* of 1054 that gave rise to the Eastern (Greek) Orthodox Church and the *Protestant Reformation* of the sixteenth and seventeenth centuries. Let's examine the changes that brought forth such powerful and long-lasting divisions within Christianity.

Before the time of Constantine's reign as Roman emperor (306–337) Christianity's primary focus was the simple truths of the gospel, the unity of believers, and proclaiming the good news of salvation to all the world. But all that changed when Constantine halted Roman persecution of Christians, decreed that Sunday was to be a national day of rest, and established Christianity as the official religion of the Roman Empire. With such a dramatic transition, the attention of the Christian Church quickly shifted to the acquisition of worldly recognition and political clout. The churches were quickly filled with people, many of them only half-converted, bringing with them their pagan rites and idolatrous practices. Consequently, there was a fusion of pagan customs with Christian beliefs that rapidly permeated all of Christianity.

Christianity's new image of public respectability and prosperity set in motion the development of a complex church structure. Intense rivalries sprang up between church leaders as each clamored for positions of power and prestige. During the fourth century, Constantine had moved the capitol of the empire from the city of Rome to Byzantium (renamed Constantinople), dividing both the Roman Empire and Christianity. The Christian leaders in these two cities, along with leaders in other major cities, aggressively competed to expand their circle of authority and influence. In time, the bishop of Rome claimed the position as the supreme leader and took the prestigious title of *pope*. That segment of Christianity over which the pope presided became known as the Roman Catholic Church.

## Shifting Spiritual Priorities

As stated in previous lessons, biblical Christianity is unique and different from all other religions in that it upholds Christ as the center of all life and our only hope of salvation. Without this premise, religion has no redemptive value. However, the inner turmoil created by escalating pagan influence and bitter power struggles within Christianity brought about a devastating change in spiritual priorities. The focus shifted from Christ-centered spirituality to a religion of human customs and authority. This new emphasis became the underlying position of the Roman Catholic Church and turned the Middle Ages into a time of unprecedented persecution and spiritual darkness, hence the term *The Dark Ages*.

As church-centered religion expanded, the darkness deepened. God's wonderful gift of salvation through faith in Christ gradually faded into the dark shadows. We must not assume, however, that the church serves no useful purpose. The Bible clearly teaches that the Christian Church was raised up and ordained of God (Matthew 16:18). Its primary purpose is to communicate the gospel to all the world and to facilitate corporate worship, fellowship, and service. And for several centuries Christianity faithfully pro-

claimed the truths of God's word and zealously responded to the needs of the people inside and outside its doors.

One of the main reasons for the church's failure to continue carrying out God's purposes is illustrated by the story of the death of Louis XIV of France and his funeral that was held in the majestic cathedral of Notre Dame. Anticipating nobility from around the world, all preparations were lavishly carried out with great pomp. The dead king was attired in the most luxurious robes, befitting the king's greatness. When the preacher ascended the pulpit to present, what everyone supposed would be a magnificent eulogy, he shocked his listeners with just four short words: "Only God is great!"

As a **human** organization, the church must ever be on guard not to take center stage and usurp the work, the authority, and greatness that is befitting of **God** alone. But that's precisely what happened! The New Testament speaks of the rise of a religious power that exalts "himself over everything that is called God or is worshiped, so that he sets himself up in God's temple, proclaiming himself to be God" (2 Thessalonians 2:4). In the Book of Revelation, this spiritual system is depicted as exercising great authority, making "war against the saints," and is repeatedly accused of blasphemy (Revelation 13:5-7), defined in Scripture as humanity taking upon itself the prerogatives of God (John 10:33). Unfortunately, speaking **for** God can easily degenerate into speaking **as** God.

History vividly bears out sin's mysterious power to awaken within the human heart aggressive ambitions for self-exaltation—to desire the highest place and covet the greatest power. Nothing distinguishes the kingdoms of the world from the kingdom of God so clearly as their opposing views of power (Mark 10:42, 43). Striving for self-centered greatness always leads to tragic consequences—in the world as well as in the church. The intense rivalry between church leaders, the ever-widening gap between clergy and laity, the emphasis on church decrees and traditions, and the savage persecution of anyone who stood in the way were just a few examples of a spiritual system that had become morally bankrupt.

## The Great Schism

When the Roman Empire was divided during Constantine's reign, it also split the Christian Church. Growing differences in language, culture, and religious beliefs caused these two divisions within Christianity to gradually drift apart. There were several key issues over which there was intense disagreement for centuries, such as the exact location of the boundaries that divided them, the veneration and use of images, the celebration of Easter, the nature of the Holy Spirit, the relationship of church and state, which writings should be included in the New Testament, and whether the clergy should be bearded or clean shaven, married or single. Perhaps the most serious conflict was the matter of ecclesiastical authority. Neither the popes of Rome nor the patriarchs of Constantinople were willing to be subservient to each other. Finally in 1054, the pope excommunicated the patriarch, a

powerful declaration that cuts the victim off from church fellowship and access to salvation. The patriarch retaliated by excommunicating the pope. The schism was now complete, a condition that exists to this day.

The word *orthodox* means "right belief." The Eastern Orthodox Church does not consider itself Roman Catholic or Protestant but somewhere in between. On the issue of salvation, however, it holds to the Roman Catholic view of the sacraments and rejects the Protestant belief of justification by faith alone. Today there are thirteen divisions within the Orthodox Church, each having its own patriarch, and all of them considered as equals. The Orthodox Church does not recognize the pope as the supreme spiritual authority, but rather, it looks to church councils as the ultimate arbiter of the Christian faith.

The Orthodox Church believes in heaven and hell but not purgatory. Although they do not worship or pray to Mary, they prominently display and reverence icons (flat images—painted mosaics of Mary and other saints) and sacred relics in their worship service. The priests, who are permitted to marry, perform the Mass in the common language while facing the congregation (something the Catholic priests did not practice until the twentieth century). The Orthodox Church has always allowed the laity to partake of the bread (leavened rather than unleavened) and the wine during Communion. Within the church there are no pews to sit on, though chairs are provided for the infirm and elderly. No matter how lengthy the worship service or whether it's a funeral or a wedding, as a sign of reverence, the worshipers are expected to remain standing.

## The Great Reformation

Eastern Orthodoxy's decision to **separate** from Roman Catholicism left the Catholic faith virtually unchanged. On the other hand, Protestantism initially determined to **reform** the Roman Catholic Church. From the eleventh to the sixteenth century, there were many voices of protest against the enormous wealth and power of Roman Catholicism, the supremacy of the papacy, and the severe enforcement of its unbiblical beliefs and practices. These voices were ignored and quickly silenced by papal threats and persecution. When the Protestant Reformation received the same response, it emerged as a powerful movement outside of Roman Catholicism, restoring many of the biblical teachings that were lost sight of during the Dark Ages.

## CHRISTIANITY

Roman Catholicism

The Reformation        Great Schism

Eastern Orthodox

Protestantism

When Benjamin Franklin wished to interest the people of Philadelphia in street lighting, he didn't try to persuade them by just talking about it. He hung a beautifully polished lantern on a long bracket in the front of his home. Every evening at the approach of dusk, he would light the wick. As the people walked or drove by his home, they discovered how wonderful it was to have the light shine on their pathway. Now they could see the sharp stones, the potholes, and the puddles of water. As others began to place lights at their homes, the city of Philadelphia soon recognized that it could no longer go without street lamps. In much the same way, Protestantism was the light bearer that was so desperately needed, not only within Christianity but also in the entire world.

There were three key issues on which Protestantism had its greatest impact and which still set the Protestant churches apart from Roman Catholicism today. The first is the matter of spiritual **authority**. Roman Catholics view tradition (church customs and pronouncements) as equal to the teachings of Scripture, with ultimate authority residing in the papacy. Consequently, a large share of the major beliefs and practices of Roman Catholicism are based on the authority of the church rather than on Scripture. This includes such doctrines as Sunday sacredness; praying to Mary and deceased saints; purgatory; the church as the official interpreter of Scripture; veneration of images and relics; celibacy of the priests; eternal torment in hell; indulgences; infant baptism; confession of sin to the priest; the Eucharist (transubstantiation); the Apocrypha as part of the Bible; the immaculate conception, assumption, and mediatorial work of Mary; and papal infallibility.

In contrast, Protestantism affirms that Scripture **alone** is the final authority for the Christian. As divine revelation, the Bible is seen as the standard by which everything else is judged. The Reformers rejected all of the above mentioned doctrines as unbibli-

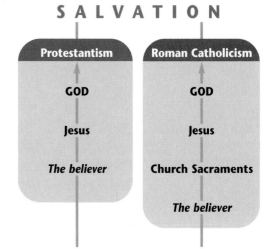

cal—with the exception of Sunday sacredness, eternal hell, and infant baptism. Later reform on these beliefs came at different times.

The second issue was the matter of **worship**—not simply its form, but its focus. Though all of the beliefs listed under the heading of authority could also apply to worship, a key doctrine that was not noted was church *sacraments*. During the Dark Ages, being saved by grace through faith alone was replaced with the mistaken idea that salvation was passed on to believers through the church. The rituals that are seen as holy channels for dispensing salvation are called sacraments. The seven sacraments that have been approved by the Roman Catholic Church can be administered only by a priest. These sacraments are infant baptism, confirmation, penance, the Eucharist (the Mass), holy orders, marriage, and anointing of the sick (last rites). So from the moment of birth to the time of one's death, the entire process of salvation within Roman Catholicism is supervised and controlled by the church.

Protestantism maintains, however, that baptism and the Communion service are the only biblical sacraments (ordinances). Ordinances are seen by Protestants more as **symbols** of how salvation **has been** personally received by the believer from Christ, rather than as **channels** by which saving grace **is being** conveyed to the believer by the church (the priests). This Protestant concept affirms the biblical doctrine of the priesthood of all believers—that each believer can communicate directly with God through Jesus Christ.

The third Roman Catholic belief that came under the attack of Protestantism was the doctrine of **salvation**, especially the relationship of faith and works. Roman Catholicism teaches that in salvation God infuses (fills) the soul (at baptism) with sanctifying grace (supernatural power), creating an inner righteousness that makes a person pleasing and acceptable to God. The repentant sinner is now committed to a lifelong process of **becoming righteous enough to achieve justification** and thus worthy of eternal life at one's death. Roman Catholics generally believe, however, that a person cannot attain, during one's lifetime, the holiness needed to qualify for heaven. Only after one has died and experienced purgatory can ultimate purity be achieved, entitling one to enter God's presence.

On the other hand, Protestantism teaches that when we as sinners exercise faith in Christ and accept Him as our Savior, Christ's perfect righteousness, already done in our behalf, is imputed (credited) to us. Protestantism views **justification as God declaring a repentant sinner righteous**, thus qualified for heaven, on the basis of the righteousness of our Substitute, Jesus Christ. Salvation is a gift we **receive** through faith; thus we must always trust in the merits of Jesus, never in our own attainments or in any goodness worked out in our lives through the Holy Spirit. The good works of a believer are not a way to **gain**

59

salvation, but rather, an expression of **gratitude** for salvation already received.

In summary, our Christian roots must be grounded in a **Person**, namely, Jesus Christ and His work of redemption freely offered to all. We must uphold salvation in Christ alone, by grace alone, through faith alone. We must reject anything that diminishes this emphasis and replaces it with church traditions or human accomplishments.

## Anchor Text

"It is by his grace you are saved, through trusting in him; it is not your own doing. It is God's gift, not a reward for work done. There is nothing for anyone to boast of. For

# Reaction

## Discussion Questions

1. Why did first-century Christians believe that Christ would return in their day? Do you believe that this was God's original plan?

2. Why did Christianity prosper and grow so rapidly in the early centuries amid such severe persecution?

3. Do you think that the Old Testament is sufficient to adequately defend the Christian faith?

4. Explain why the truths of God's Word can be understood in such conflicting ways.

5. Are there any Christian doctrines that do not seem to amplify or make real Christ's love and His saving grace?

6. The lesson states that when Christianity became the official religion of the Roman Empire, the churches were filled with people "only half-converted." What is a half-converted Christian?

7. Why do you think Sunday observance, eternal hell fire, and infant baptism have remained within Protestantism to the present time?

8. What is your definition of *Christianity*?

## Personal Response

Is your life Christ centered or church (friends) centered? Is your view of salvation clear and simple or complicated and ambiguous? Is your faith biblically based, or does it simply reflect your own ideas and opinions? Take the time to write out a brief and concise statement that describes your Christian faith and the Bible texts on which it is based.

we are God's handiwork, created in Christ Jesus to devote ourselves to the good deeds for which God has designed us" (Ephesians 2:8-10, NEB).

## Bible Search

One of the objectives of the Seventh-day Adventist Church is to recapture the simplicity and the focus of the early Christian Church. Read Acts 2:22-47 and Acts 4:8-12, which clearly describe the original beliefs and practices of the first Christians. (A) List these beliefs and practices as you read these verses of Scripture. (B) Which of these do you think are most needed within our church today?

## Practical Application

1. Interview five people (including teenagers and adults) and ask them to define *Christianity*. Write out their answers and conclude the assignment with your personal reaction to what you heard and saw. When all the students have shared their responses with the class, choose the two or three responses you believe are the most accurate or insightful.

2. In the early centuries Christians had to "clearly define" the content or essence of their faith. Get into groups of three or four students and come to a mutual agreement as to what you believe are the five most important beliefs of Christianity today. Each group is to share its list with the rest of the class.

3. This is a spiritual-roots inventory. Interview your parents and find out how long they have been members of the Seventh-day Adventist Church or whatever church they belong to. What were the reasons and the circumstances for becoming Seventh-day Adventists? What were they before becoming Seventh-day Adventists? How many generations in your family were Seventh-day Adventists? If your grandparents are available, perhaps you could ask them the same questions. Along with your completed interviews, write your personal reactions to what you found out. Be prepared to share this report with the class.

4. Select one of the following topics and write a 350-word research paper:
   A. Describe either the basic beliefs, practices, or the worship service of the Eastern Orthodox Church. Attend a worship service and interview one of the church members or simply interview a priest or church member.
   B. Explain the theological significance of the Roman Catholic Eucharist (Mass) and how it differs from the Protestant Communion service. If possible, attend a Roman Catholic Mass and interview the priest or a church member regarding the meaning of the service to them.

A person without knowledge of his or her history is like a tree without roots.

# Keeping Protest Alive

Choices can often overwhelm us! For example, if you were to choose a Christian denomination in the United States, do you know that there are at least 202 possibilities?[1] With such a wide array of denominations, what's the need for the Seventh-day Adventist Church? Wouldn't it simplify things if Christians were simply known as Catholics, Protestants, and Orthodox and ignored all the other labels? Let's explore some possible answers.

## The Reformation: Only the Beginning

Two neighbors were engaged in a friendly chat when one made the following comment: "I have a friend who considers herself a born-again Christian, yet I know that she cheats on her husband. How do you explain that?" Her friend came back with this interesting reply, "I'd say she was a born-again Christian with birth defects." In a world of sin and imperfection, it seems that whatever we do is flawed in some way. Our best efforts will always be incomplete and fall short of God's ideal.

The same is true for the Protestant Reformation. During the Middle Ages, religion was closely tied to every aspect of life. In fact, spiritual beliefs were so interwoven with one's everyday life and cultural heritage that a complete reformation could not possibly have taken place at once. Clearly, the Reformation dramatically altered Christianity's focus, but it was only the beginning. There were many other issues that had not been recognized and addressed. Since spiritual awareness and growth often come slowly, God in His mercy will not allow so much light to shine upon our pathway that we become overwhelmed or discouraged. Jesus made this clear to His disciples when He said, "I have much more to say to you, more than you can now bear. But when he, the Spirit of truth, comes, he will guide you into all truth" (John 16:12, 13).

## Reactions to the Reformation

There were three general ways that people initially responded to the Protestant Reformation. First, there were those who opposed the Protestant movement and everything it stood for. Second, there were those who wholeheartedly joined the movement, agreeing in principle with its basic beliefs and objectives. The third group were those who supported the Reformation but thought that it hadn't gone far enough. Let's examine these groups more closely.

**The Opposition:** Roman Catholicism's opposition to the Protestant Reformation was most forcefully carried out through the Counter-Reformation. This movement was given a powerful thrust by the Council of

Trent, a gathering of Roman Catholic leaders for twenty-five sessions between 1545 to 1563. Though it initiated some minor reforms, it staunchly upheld **all** the traditional (unbiblical) doctrines of the Roman Catholic Church that had been challenged by the Protestants. The decrees of this council eventually became the basic premise of the official teachings of modern Catholicism. The objectives of the Counter-Reformation were carried out by the untiring efforts of the Jesuits, by the publication of *The Index of Prohibited Books* (purportedly listing 75 percent of all books in print in Europe at the time), and by the papal Inquisition (the search for and severe punishment of heretics).

**The Supporters:** Martin Luther's posting of The Ninety-Five Theses (a public condemnation of Indulgences) in 1517 ignited the Protestant Reformation, sending shock waves throughout Europe. As other powerful

reformers emerged, adding their voices to the rising tide of protest, massive numbers of people joined the movement. Luther established a *Lutheran* base in Germany, Calvin developed the *Reformed* faith in France, and the *Anglican* movement sprang to life in England. However, only the Lutherans and the Reformed were in general agreement as to the key pillars of the Reformation.

use of candles and the crucifix in the worship service, affirming the bodily presence of Christ with the bread and wine, and allowing the church to be under the control of civil authorities. Supervision of each local church by a ruling prince often stifled personal and congregational reform.

The **Reformed Church** (also known as Presbyterian) emphasized holiness of life

| Pillars of the Reformation | | |
|---|---|---|
| | *Sola Scriptura:* | The Bible **alone** is the ultimate authority. |
| | *Sola Christos:* | Salvation is in Christ **alone**. |
| | *Sola Gratis:* | Salvation comes by grace **alone**. |
| | *Sola Fide:* | Justification comes through faith **alone**. |

As the Reformation grew and expanded, more differences began to emerge between these Protestant groups, resulting in further subdivisions known as denominations. Although disputes involved doctrinal matters, they especially focused on church liturgy—prescribed rites for public worship, and on church government—the issue of organization and authority.

In the **Lutheran Church**, the emphasis turned from performing the Mass to preaching the Word, with the entire worship service spoken in German rather than Latin. All worshipers participated in the Communion service that was held at each worship service, and congregational singing replaced the chanting of the priests. Though Lutherans revitalized Christianity as no one else had done in over 1,000 years, yet they were often censured for not going far enough in their reforms. They were criticized for continuing some Catholic practices, such as the

and eagerly applied the principles of the gospel to the whole life of society. It promoted the sovereignty of God, and with it came the idea of predestination and irresistible grace (that God chooses who will be saved and lost). It chose a *presbyterian* form of church government, a system based on representative groups of *presbyters* (elders) that have ascending levels of authority and responsibility. The fact that the Reformed faith was essentially a complementary movement to Lutheranism greatly strengthened the Protestant Reformation.

The **Anglican Church** (also known as the Church of England) initially emerged as the result of a heated dispute between Henry VIII and the Roman Catholic Church regarding his right to divorce the first of his six wives. Only after this issue was resolved, with the king becoming the supreme head of the Church, did a long and tedious process of spiritual and cultural change begin. At first, the Church of England adopted an *episcopal* form of church government, in which the king replaced the pope as the head of the Church. Today the episcopalian system is based on a hierarchical organization, in which the clergy and the local churches are supervised by bishops.

**The Radicals:** Those who firmly believed that Protestantism was not moving fast enough or far enough ignited the *Radical Reformation*. These reformers were painfully aware that many unbiblical beliefs and practices still remained unchallenged and unchanged. Perhaps one of the most glaring weaknesses of Protestantism was the continuation of the Roman Catholic practice of state or "established" churches. Civil authorities were used to empower Reformation churches, while placing a ban on all minority groups. Reformation churches became national churches that legislated their religious views and enforced them on their adherents. In other words, **spiritual correction** was followed by **civil coercion**. Religious freedom so often taken for granted in the United States was not an immediate outcome of the Protestant Reformation.

Perhaps the strongest voice within the Radical Reformation was the **Anabaptists**, generally viewed as the fourth major group to emerge from Protestantism. Anabaptists were so named because they rejected infant baptism and chose to be rebaptized. Based on their understanding of the New Testament, they adamantly opposed the state's influencing church decisions and enforcing church doctrines. Undoubtedly, large numbers of people had joined the Protestant movement out of commitment to civil rulers rather than from conversion to Jesus Christ. Besides opposing a state church and affirming that each local church was to be self-governing *(congregationalism)*, Anabaptists also supported pacifism, opposed oaths and capital punishment, and upheld the New Testament teaching of the believer's baptism.

Although there were different kinds of Anabaptists, they were all generally viewed as subversive and dangerous extremists by Protestants and Catholics alike, and thousands of them died as martyrs at the hands of fellow Christians. The Anabaptist attempt to keep the spirit of protest alive clearly demonstrates that it was a daring and costly venture.

**Reformation Needs Revival**

Generally speaking, the words *reformation* and *revival* tend to be used interchangeably. In this lesson, however, *reformation* refers to the **restoration** of spiritual truths that have been lost while *revival* points to the **regeneration** of spiritual life that has tapered off. In other words, reformation focuses on truth; revival, on love. Truth without love is cold and oppressive, while love without truth is spiritual zeal without direction. Obviously, reformation and revival are equally important.

It did not take long for the Reformation to begin losing much of its original zeal and passionate commitment. Its progress and influence were greatly stymied by the Counter-Reformation, led by the aggressive efforts of the Jesuits. Internal feuds and rivalries made Protestants extremely conscious of doctrinal differences and thus preoccupied with formulating doctrinal creeds. This emphasis often produced cold, scholarly documents of belief, with very little appeal to conversion and heartfelt joy, warmth, and devotion.

## Truth without love is cold and oppressive, while love without truth is spiritual zeal without direction.

There was also a growing misunderstanding of "justification by faith alone." Some reasoned that since good works do not contribute to one's salvation, then why be zealous in doing good? All of these issues were relentlessly sapping Protestantism of its initial momentum for Christ-centered reform and bringing the movement nearly to a standstill. There was an urgent need for revival, a rekindling of the fervor and wholeheartedness it once had.

This illustrates an important truth: We are either growing or dying, advancing or regressing. The Bible declares that our lamps are either burning brightly, or they're going out. God is not pleased with a flickering light! To the church in Sardis, a church generally viewed as representing the Protestant Reformation era, the angel declares, "I know your deeds; you have a reputation of being alive, but you are dead. Wake up! Strengthen what remains and is about to die, for I have

not found your deeds complete in the sight of my God" (Revelation 3:1, 2). As God had raised up voices to protest Roman Catholic doctrine, there was a need for new voices to challenge the waning spirit of Protestantism.

During the seventeenth, eighteenth, and nineteenth centuries, Protestantism experienced a great deal of change and renewal. Although this was accomplished by scores of different groups, we will focus on only four movements:

- **Puritanism** and **Separatism** in England.
- **Pietism** in Germany.
- **Methodism** and the **Awakenings** in America.
- **The Advent Movement** in America.

### A Time of Separation

*Puritans* and *Separatists* had their greatest impact within the Anglican Church. Puritans had very little confidence in traditional religion and church rituals. They stressed human sinfulness, upholding the need for the new birth and maintaining that the believer should give evidence of this experience by living a holy life. Emphasis was given to church discipline and high moral standards, such as strict observance of Sunday, church attendance, Bible reading, and purity of thought and language.

At first the Puritans did not oppose "state" churches, but eventually they opted for a presbyterian form of church government, insisting that Christ alone should be considered the Head of the church. Those who preferred a congregational form of church government and demanded a complete separation of church and state became known as Separatists. It was their objective to abolish everything in Protestantism that hinted of Roman Catholic belief or practice. Convinced that such reforms would never take place, they chose to separate from the Church of England, hence the term *Separatists.* Strangely enough, when the Puritans and Separatists came to America, they set up a theocratic form of civil government in which dissenters were again persecuted.

### The Arrival of Pietism

Around 1670 a young Lutheran preacher by the name of Philip Spener, alarmed by the spiritual apathy of his people, began holding house meetings for those who desired a deeper study of God's Word. It didn't take long until these meetings were scornfully called "gatherings of the pious," hence the term *Pietism.* It quickly became a renewal movement within Lutheranism, emphasizing home Bible study and calling for an end to Protestant disputes and for preaching that focused on repentance and holy living. Pietism shifted the emphasis from controversy to caring, from creeds to conversion, from mandatory worship services to voluntary fellowship groups. From this movement came the *Brethren,* one of the very few denominations that still practices ceremonial foot washing today.

The changes created by Pietism were essential, but as the revival grew, in some places it became imbalanced. Endeavoring to get away from intellectualism, there was an overemphasis on experience and emotion. Not wanting to become embroiled in doctrinal disputes resulted in too little atten-tion being given to Scripture.

Spiritual balance is just as crucial today as it was centuries ago. Just as the Word and Spirit each have an essential role in salvation, so religion must appeal equally to the head and the heart, to the intellect and the emotions. There is a common tendency for churches to emphasize one at the expense of the other. Feelings of joy, love, sorrow, or

**Just as the Word and Spirit each have an essential role in salvation, so religion must appeal equally to the head and the heart, to the intellect and the emotions.**

compassion are vital in worship and in our daily walk with God. But emotions are often fleeting and easily manipulated; thus people can be readily deceived or led astray by that which appeals to the senses. Jesus rebuked the Jews, saying, "None of you will ever believe unless you see miracles and wonders" (John 4:48, TEV). Feelings must always be examined in light of God's Word to determine whether they are healthy and holy.

### The Rise of Methodism

During a closing meeting of an academy week of prayer, several students stood up to give public expression to their faith and what Christ meant to them. Eventually a young girl reluctantly stood to her feet, and with tears streaming down her cheeks, she said, "I know I need to give my heart to God. But I don't expect to have another day of fun in my life."

Mistaken notions about the Christian life are nothing new. By the time of the eighteenth century, the Enlightenment, humanism, deism, and the Industrial Revolution caused many to turn away from religion in Europe and America. With Puritan influence nearly extinct, those who belonged to the Church of England, which was one of the major churches in the colonies, were in desperate need of revival.

John Wesley, the founder of Methodism, was an Anglican clergyman who quickly discovered that denunciation of society's sins and the call for repentance was not readily received by his church. Spurned by the Anglican clergy, Wesley chose to speak in crowded jails, aboard sailing ships, and in open fields. By the time his preaching career ended some fifty years later, he had nearly 80,000 followers in England and 40,000 in America. The "Methodists" eventually separated from the Anglican Church in 1784 and became a new denomination, the Methodist Episcopal Church. Today there are thirteen different churches within Methodism, the largest being the United Methodist Church with nearly 10 million members.

The impact of Methodism was significant. First, it proved to be a definite answer to the social ills of its day. It effectively countered the influence of deism in England. It met the needs of the downtrodden working class in the cities, for whom the Anglican Church did relatively nothing. It played a major role in guarding England from some of the political upheaval that France suffered during the French Revolution. It provided for medical dispensaries, orphanages, and relief for the poor. It led the way in prison reform, the abolition of slavery in England, and regulating working conditions by enforcing work codes and child labor laws.

Second, Methodism was an "experiential" religion, a religion of the heart. It was a religion of revival, emphasizing the need for inner growth and Christian perfection. Christians were viewed as having received **pardon** in order to **participate** with the Holy Spirit in the work of sanctification, a cleansing of the soul from all sin, leaving only an inner purity, peace, and power to do God's will. For Methodists, sanctification provided the fruits of the Spirit that empowered the believer to be more useful in God's service and more effective in converting the world to God.

Third, the most dominant Protestant force in America during the latter years of the eighteenth century and the early part of the nineteenth was Methodism, thus becoming known as "the Methodist Age." America's first major revival, the Great Awakening from 1720–1760, preceded this time period. This revival awakened an anti-slavery sentiment, actively resisted the idea of state-controlled churches, and promoted the idea of denominations—churches within Christianity having equal status. The Second Great Awakening (1800–1830) was characterized by the use of camp meetings, a distinctive Methodist feature. People from a wide region would gather together in the woods or meadow and spend several days attending revival meetings. These highly emotional gatherings, lasting far into the night, usually ended with people walking down "the sawdust trail" and making things right with

however, that Seventh-day Adventism's rich spiritual heritage extends back to many other segments of Protestantism. It has built on the foundations previously laid by generations of reform movements and Christian denominations.

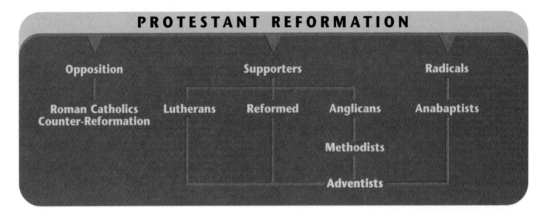

**PROTESTANT REFORMATION**

| Opposition | Supporters | Radicals |
|---|---|---|
| Roman Catholics Counter-Reformation | Lutherans | Reformed | Anglicans | Anabaptists |

Methodists

Adventists

God at the "mourner's bench." An important outgrowth of this revival was bringing the gospel to the unchurched pioneers, the Native Americans, and the slaves.

### The Role of Adventism

The Advent Movement sprang into existence at the height of Methodism in America. In fact, Ellen White was a Methodist before she became a Millerite. Adventism's early emphasis on heartfelt religious experience and Christian perfection also characterized Methodism. Adventist preaching on the need to trust in Jesus for salvation was likewise a popular Methodist belief. By the 1840s Methodism had become America's largest Protestant denomination. Its use of camp meetings and its promotion of evangelism and "altar calls" were also early trademarks of Adventists. It should be made clear,

In this lesson we see that protest and reformation must always be ongoing. We have observed this as successive movements painstakingly uncovered biblical truths that had been long forgotten. On the other hand, Protestantism has also been guilty of complacency, too often depending on creeds or theological positions that were hammered out long ago. Such a detrimental attitude can be found in all denominations, including the Seventh-day Adventist Church.

How does the Seventh-day Adventist Church fit into the overall picture of Christianity? What do we see as our role? What is our contribution to Christianity? If our church did not exist, what difference would it make?

The Seventh-day Adventist Church sees itself as a prophetic movement raised up by

God to finish the task originally given to the disciples and to complete the work of the Reformation. It sees its mission as proclaiming the gospel within the context of the three angels' messages, making it relevant to the decisive issues of the great controversy. Seventh-day Adventism calls attention to biblical concepts that profoundly affect one's view of God and provide crucial insights to end-time events.

At the very heart of Seventh-day Adventism is the eternal gospel that centers on the saving work of Jesus Christ. The primary purpose of every doctrine is to enhance our understanding of Christ and our relationship with Him. As our name implies, Seventh-day Adventists believe that the gospel is to be proclaimed within the context of the imminent return of Jesus and the sanctity of the Sabbath. The recovery of the Sabbath truth within Christianity not only serves as a precious reminder of the "rest" the believer has in Jesus, but it is a powerful denial of evolution, a godless hypothesis of so many worldviews, religions, and philosophies. It also highlights the supremacy of Scriptural authority—the basis for Sabbath sacredness, over against human authority—the basis for Sunday observance.

In proclaiming God's free gift of grace lavished upon us at Calvary, Seventh-day Adventists acknowledge this as the very core of the Christian faith. They also believe that this glorious truth will be attacked, discarded, and perverted into a righteousness-by-works religion just as it was during the Dark Ages. Apostate religion of the last days will also be marked by two other prominent errors—the enforced observance of Sunday and the belief in the immortality of the soul.

In our day the Seventh-day Adventist Church must not only uplift the significance of the Sabbath, it must also point out to the world that humankind is not immortal by nature, thus eliminating the reality of an eternal hell, purgatory, reincarnation, and spiritualism—supposed communication with the dead. The danger of such unbiblical teachings is twofold: First, God is viewed as a hideous tyrant whose justice demands and delights in the eternal suffering of the lost. It makes God the most abusive Parent in the universe! Second, these errors are attractive doorways to involvement with the occult and the demonic realm. Consequently, God warns us that apostate religion of the last days will be "a home for demons and a haunt for every evil spirit" (Revelation 18:2). What an indictment of end-time spirituality! What a mandate for God's end-time people to keep "protest" alive!

## Anchor Text

"Since we are surrounded by such a great cloud of witnesses, let us throw off everything that hinders and the sin that so easily entangles, and let us run with perseverance the race marked out for us. Let us fix our eyes on Jesus, the author and perfecter of our faith" (Hebrews 12:1, 2).

**NOTES**

1. Frank S. Mead and Samuel S. Hill. *Handbook of Denominations in the United States*, New ninth edition (Nashville, Tenn.: Abingdon Press, 1992).

**WRITER ACKNOWLEDGMENT OF RESOURCES**

Horton, Michael S., ed. *Power Religion.* (Chicago, Ill.: Moody Press, 1992).

Schneider, Gregory. "The *Methodist* Connection to *Adventism.*" *Spectrum*, vol. 25, number 5 (September 1996), pages 26-37.

Whidden, Woodrow. "Ellen White and John Wesley." *Spectrum*, vol. 25, number 5 (September 1996), pages 48-54.

### Bible Search

1. What does "keeping protest alive" mean to you? Do you see yourself as the "oppo-

# Reaction

72

## Discussion Questions

1. What correlation do you see between the pace of the Reformation and the rate of spiritual growth in your own life?

2. Why did it take so long for the idea of voluntary worship and religious freedom to become a Christian practice?

3. Which form of church government do you think makes the most sense—episcopalian, presbyterian, or congregationalism? Explain your answer.

4. Is it reformation or revival that is most needed in our church? Why?

5. How would you answer this question: If good works do not contribute to salvation, why then be zealous in doing good?

6. Why might people think that they will not have any fun if they become Christians?

7. What would you say are the most important contributions of the Seventh-day Adventist Church to Christianity or the world?

sition," a "supporter," or perhaps a "radical" to spiritual reform? As a follower of Christ, what sins in your life should you be protesting against? What personal reforms should you be advocating? Read Colossians 3:1-25 and list at least ten spiritual goals that God holds out to you.

2. Select two or three spiritual goals listed in question 1 that are most needful in your life and devise a plan that spans the next two weeks as to how these aspects will be strengthened or incorporated into your daily life.

## Personal Response

It's always difficult to be radical when it comes to our everyday walk with Jesus Christ. Since reformation doesn't happen all at once, what "radical" changes are you willing to let Jesus accomplish for you in your life?

## Practical Application

1. Write a two-minute TV commercial for the Seventh-day Adventist Church.

2. Attend a Lutheran, Episcopal, Presbyterian, or Methodist church service. Your visitation will be probably more enjoyable if two or three of you go together. Write a 350-word report that includes a description of the visitation as well as an interview with at least one member of the church. You may wish to take a video camera with you in doing your interview.

3. Divide into small groups and discuss and answer the questions on the worksheet "What Do You Mean—Seventh-day Adventist?" provided by your teacher.

4. Write a 350-word paper describing the appropriate balance that should exist between head knowledge (doctrinal belief) and heartfelt emotion in the Christian life. Your teacher will provide you with a list of some resource materials.

Woe to the person who opens God's Word expecting to learn nothing new.

# Lesson 8

# The Protestant Progeny

They lived just across the river from us—all seventeen of them—the parents and their fifteen children. The children ranged in age from one to twenty-four, and it seemed that I never saw the entire family together at any one time. I was told that one day a salesman drove into the yard just as the mother was calling the family to dinner. The salesman could hardly believe his eyes as he saw kids running from every direction toward the front door of the house. One little fellow had the misfortune, however, of stumbling and falling flat on his face. After a few moments he got up, dusted himself off, and started walking back to the place he had just left. "Hey, Sonny," the salesman called out, "aren't you going to eat dinner?"

"Are you kidding?" came back the reply. "By now the food's all gone!"

I suppose that in a family that large, with such a wide range in ages, it's quite likely that the younger children really never got to know some of the older ones. The unusual size of this family illustrates a problem that also holds true for "the great family of God" (Ephesians 3:15, TLB). Protestant progeny—descendants or disciples—constitute a worldwide assortment of denominations of which we may know very little or perhaps nothing at all. All of us have friends, relatives, neighbors, or other people that we meet who are not Seventh-day Adventists. Knowing something about their religious beliefs can be very helpful when sharing with them your own spiritual faith.

At this point let's define some terms we will be using in this lesson:

## PROTESTANTISM

As a major division within Christianity, Protestantism is divided into smaller organizations as noted below.

## DENOMINATIONS

**Adventist, Baptist, Episcopal, Lutheran, Mennonite, Methodist, Pentecostal, Presbyterian, Reformed**

These are examples of some of the larger Protestant denominations. Each of these are further subdivided into smaller church groups. Listed below are some examples of different kinds of Adventist groups that exist today.

## CHURCHES

**Seventh-day Adventist, Advent Christian Church, Church of God Seventh Day**

It is a common practice to also refer to these church groups as denominations. Within each of these church groups are local church congregations. For example:

## CONGREGATIONS

**Loma Linda University Church, Dakota**

Adventist Academy Church, Sligo Seventh-day Adventist Church

## Common Protestant Bonds

The Protestant groups that emerged out of the Reformation differed from one another primarily in the extent of their departure from Roman Catholicism and their return to apostolic Christianity. In other words, while some reformers made relatively few changes, others were determined to turn away from everything that seemed Roman Catholic. As Protestants fled to America, where religious freedom became a prominent feature, divisions among Protestants became even more commonplace. Before we examine these divisions, let's note some areas of mutual agreement. Most Protestants today generally subscribe, to a greater or lesser degree, to the following:

- A transcendent, personal God who created all things.
- The Trinity—the equality of the Father, Son, and Holy Spirit.
- Salvation from sin through grace alone.
- The Bible as divine revelation and man's primary authority.
- The church as divinely appointed for worship, fellowship, and witness.
- The biblical ordinances of baptism and the Communion service.
- Sunday as the "Lord's day"—the day of worship.
- The immortality of the soul and eternal punishment of the lost.
- The priesthood of all believers.
- The imperative of living the Christian life.

- The judgment, resurrection, and Second Coming.

There are other areas of general consent, but these are examples of the more important ones. Seventh-day Adventists agree with all these except Sunday observance, the immortality of the soul, and eternal punishment, which we believe are not based on Scripture.

## American Protestantism

American Protestantism has often been divided into three general categories. Many of the older, more liberal denominations, such as Lutheran, Reformed, Presbyterian, and Episcopalian, are commonly referred to as *mainline Protestantism*. A large share of the churches within these denominations emphasize a highly formal worship service carried out by the clergy, adhere to historical creeds, and promote tolerance. *Evangelicalism* represents a more conservative kind of Protestantism that is found both within and outside of mainline Protestantism. To be evangelical means to proclaim the good news of the gospel. Evangelicals also emphasize the new birth, holiness of life, and Bible study; and they favor more informal worship services. The Baptists are a prime example of Evangelicals. *Fundamentalism* is the most conservative division of Protestantism, calling for a return to "fundamental" beliefs—such as the literal interpretation of the Bible, creationism, the imminence of the second coming of Christ (and the "secret rapture")—and taking a strong stand against worldliness. Holiness and Pentecostal churches emphasize being born again in the

Spirit, accompanied by speaking in tongues. Worship services are characterized by faith healing, personal testimonies, spontaneous prayer and dancing, and upraised arms and shouts of praise. In recent years, some fundamentalists, generally referred to as the "Christian right," have become politically active in promoting social issues, such as pro-life, prayer in public schools, federal aid for religious education, and traditional family values.

There are definite drawbacks in putting denominations into specific categories. For example, some churches, like the Seventh-day Adventist Church, might fit into more than one category. Some interdenominational community congregations or prominent TV evangelistic organizations don't seem to fit into any of the slots. Some of the most conservative denominations, such as the Mennonites and Amish, are very different from the conservatism of Pentecostal churches or the political activism of the "Christian right." We need to recognize the limited value of religious labels.

### Protestant Churches Today

In Protestantism every denomination wants more than a label. Just as each child in a family wants to be recognized for his or her unique qualities, the same holds true for churches. And in a large family, some siblings may have left home even before the younger ones were born. With this in mind, let's take a look at some of the older and younger members of American Protestantism and highlight a few of their unique characteristics.

**Lutheran:** Lutherans were the firstborn. At the start they simply wanted to be known as Christians or Evangelicals. "Lutheran" was originally a derisive nickname given by Catholics for the "heresy" of Luther and his followers, but today it is a name of honor and is greatly respected for its religious tradition.

There are nine different Lutheran bodies in the United States, making Lutheranism the third largest Protestant denomination in the United States. Lutherans do not define themselves by their organizational structure (which ranges from episcopalian to congregational) but by their creeds. *The Book of*

## In Protestantism every denomination wants more than a label.

*Concord*, published in 1580, is a collection of their earliest creeds that still serves as an authoritative source of Lutheran beliefs. Though Lutheranism today still reflects a great deal of Catholic liturgy, its primary mission is the preaching of the gospel—that we are saved by grace alone through faith alone. It administers the two biblical sacraments, upholds the Bible as the ultimate standard, and fosters a comprehensive educational system for its members. To accomplish its mission, the Lutheran church maintains the second largest parochial (religious) school system in America. (Seventh-day Adventists rank third; however it ranks number two in the world, second only to Roman Catholicism).

**Reformed and Presbyterian:** These twin denominations came to life in the late sixteenth century through the efforts of John Calvin and John Knox respectively. In America today there are eight Reformed bodies and six Presbyterian groups, each of them based on a presbyterian (representative) form of church government. Both denominations base their beliefs on the Bible as interpreted and clarified by creeds, and they conduct formal worship services, though much simpler than Lutheran or Episcopalian services. They accept the two sacraments of baptism and the Lord's Supper but do not regard them as having any power in themselves. They place greater emphasis on the preaching of God's Word than the Lutherans do, believing that such preaching gives the sacraments their force and significance.

Much of their doctrinal structure revolves around the concept of sovereignty: the sovereignty of God in the universe, the sovereignty of Christ in salvation, the sovereignty of Scripture in faith and practice, and the sovereignty of the individual conscience in interpreting God's Word. Reformed and Presbyterian churches emphasize tolerance and the need for interdenominational fellowship of Protestant churches.

**Episcopalian:** The Episcopal Church is the continuation in America of the Anglican Church (Church of England). It became a powerful church within the Colonies and was known as the Church of England until the American Revolution, after which time it broke away from the mother church and became a separate organization. Of all Protestant denominations, the Episcopal Church is the closest today to the spirit and practice of Roman Catholicism. In fact, some Episcopalians see themselves as Anglican Catholics. It has an episcopal (hierarchical) church organization, with the Archbishop of Canterbury serving as head of the church. The bishops serve as the primary overseers while the priests minister to the laity, celebrate holy Communion, and pronounce absolution (forgiveness).

The Episcopalian worship services are divided into "high" and "low" church. A "high" church follows the Catholic tradition of an elaborate worship service and subscribes to seven sacraments. The high church has a view of the Mass that is very similar to that held by Roman Catholicism. The "low" church is a much more simple worship service, with an emphasis on the Protestant view of the gospel and experiential religion.

**Society of Friends**, generally known as the **Quakers**, demanded a lot more changes than their older Protestant siblings. Founded by Puritan George Fox in England in 1652, the Quakers, along with the Mennonites and Amish, reflected the radical reforms of the Anabaptists. Fox had no respect for the creeds, beliefs, and practices of the churches of his day; thus the Quakers call themselves a "society" rather than a church. They have no ministers, ceremonies, preaching, or singing. They believe that Christians should not be under any spiritual authority other than the Holy Spirit. In their worship services they sit in silence until a member of the congregation is moved by the Spirit to speak. It is their conviction that the "Inner

Light" provided by the Spirit is more reliable than the teachings of the church or even the Scripture. Views such as this tend to cast a shadow on much of their work. Today's Quakers are strongly pacifist and are actively involved in all kinds of social reforms, as well as in providing relief in times of war and disasters.

**Mennonite:** During the middle of the sixteenth century, Menno Simons, an Anabaptist refugee, single-handedly brought many of the scattered and persecuted Anabaptists together into one group. Named after him, they are today the largest denomination of direct descendants of the Anabaptists, with a worldwide membership of about 850,000 members in sixty-eight countries.

The Mennonites' main focus is to be a biblical people. It is their belief that Jesus is not only our Savior who died for us, but as our Lord, He exemplified in His earthly life the way we are to live in today's world. They view their church, which is congregational, as the primary vehicle for biblical interpretation, as well as the rightful administrator of high moral standards and strict discipline.

Today there are thirteen Mennonite groups, but perhaps the most significant split among the Mennonites took place in 1693 over the issue of church discipline. Led by Jakob Amman, those who desired greater faithfulness to biblical principles became known as the **Amish**. There are records of the Amish in America as early as 1727, and they have now spread over twenty-three states and Canada. The Amish have no central organization, do not pay their ministers a salary, and conduct very informal but

deliberate worship services. The trademark for which the Amish are known is their very plain and austere lifestyle, which represents their attempt to carry forth the Anabaptist tradition of entire separation from the world.

**Baptist:** Baptists generally do not view themselves as a denomination because of their emphasis on congregationalism—separate autonomy for each local congregation. Though their origin can be traced back to an exiled Anabaptist congregation in Amsterdam, Holland, in 1609, they see themselves as developing out of the Puritan and Separatist movement. With such a heritage, we can understand why Baptists so staunchly maintained that the Bible alone should be the Christian's guide in all things. This led to the Baptists' historic break with traditional Protestantism over infant baptism, declaring that it was not scriptural and that baptism by immersion was to be a personal expression of one's faith in Jesus Christ. Though Baptists have generally insisted on complete separation of church and state, there are recent indications that this position is being modified. With the majority of the world's thirty-five million Baptists living in the United States, it is today the largest and perhaps the most influential Protestant group in our country.

**Methodist:** While the Episcopalians decided to **retain** the traditions of the Anglican Church, the Methodists chose to **detach** themselves from what they believed were dried up spiritual roots. As was stated in the previous lesson, Methodism's original objective was not to reformulate Protestant doctrine but to **revive** the experience of

God's justifying grace and **renew** the call for Scriptural holiness. Methodism, however, has gone through a great deal of transformation since its inception in the late eighteenth century. Having divided into thirteen church groups, the clarion call to experience a new life in Christ Jesus rather than to merely pay lip service to historic creeds is no longer being sounded as unitedly as in earlier times. A primary agenda of modern Methodism is the *social gospel*—taking a direct, active interest in helping the poor and the oppressed and working for social justice. What characterized Methodism in the days of John Wesley—the preaching of the gospel that not only changed individual lives but also brought about social reforms— still lies at the heart of Methodism today.

**Pentecostal:** Pentecostalism is a vast and sprawling movement that came into being as a reaction to Protestantism's liberal turn at the very beginning of the twentieth century. A distinctive belief of Pentecostalism is that conversion to Christ will be followed by the baptism of the Holy Spirit, evidenced by glossolalia—speaking in an unknown tongue. Other external signs of Pentecostal spirituality are manifested by such spiritual gifts as divine healing, miracles, and direct revelation from God. In contrast to **performance**-oriented worship of many traditional Protestant churches, Pentecostal worship is **participation**-oriented, characterized by spontaneous waving of uplifted hands, shouting, dancing, and of course, speaking in tongues.

At first Pentecostalism's greatest influence was within Evangelicalism, with scores of

new churches emerging. In the past generation, Pentecostal distinctives have penetrated mainline Protestantism, as well as the Roman Catholic Church, often labeled as "*Charismatic Renewal.*" Another change within Pentecostalism has been a shifting of focus from a Christ-centered gospel to the pursuit of health, wealth, and worldly success, a "prosperity gospel" most noticeably trumpeted by Pentecostal televangelists. This disturbing trend is one that more traditional Pentecostals would like to see come to an end.

## The Changing Face of Protestantism

Several significant trends are presently taking place within Protestantism. Not only is culture playing a more significant role, but increasingly, Protestants are identifying more readily with social concerns and worship styles than with doctrinal issues. It is becoming apparent that when choosing a church, many people see religious traditions and liturgies as empty and useless. Spirituality marked by freedom, tolerance, and independence is rapidly replacing religion that is ceremonial and formal. This is evidenced by a high rate of membership loss in most mainline Protestant churches.

So where are people going? Many are turning to Evangelical and Fundamentalist churches, believing that what is found there is more meaningful and speaks to their needs. Some are joining "fringe" or "alternative" religions, sometimes referred to as *cults*, often submitting to a rigid lifestyle when convinced of its purpose and importance. Others are becoming members of large interdenominational community churches, where successful marketing approaches are employed to develop "user-friendly" churches. Well-orchestrated drama and musical extravaganzas are used to reach out to unchurched affluent middle-class suburbanites. Many of these churches have become so large that they are referred to as *megachurches*, churches with more than a thousand members. Twenty years ago there were 100 megachurches; today there are over 4,000.

## What Does It All Mean?

It's obvious that Protestantism is characterized by division and diversity. Is that good or bad? While some view it as a sign of spiritual weakness, others see it as positive and desirable. The Bible clearly teaches the importance of Christian unity. We are "all baptized by one Spirit into one body" (1 Corinthians 12:13). The unity of believers finds its source in the fact that there is but "one Lord, one faith, one baptism; one God and Father of us all" (Ephesians 4:5, 6). In union with Christ through the Holy Spirit, believers are united to one another, enabling them to **work together** for the salvation of the world and to **live together** in a world torn apart by culture, race, gender, and status. Unity on earth is one of the greatest evidences of the reality of God's heavenly kingdom.

There are those who mistakenly think that unity simply means uniformity (enforced compliance). The unity that believers have in Christ, however, allows for wholesome diversity in worship styles, church organization, and biblical under-

standing. The scriptural metaphor of the human body clearly illustrates that unity can exist within diversity. The body has many diverse organs and members, all receiving nourishment from the same source, all working together to maintain the body's health and proper functions, yet each one carrying out a vital, though different, task. Likewise, the Christian Church with all its diversity must unitedly stand under the Lordship of Christ if it is to effectively reach out and proclaim the gospel "to every nation, tribe, language and people" (Revelation 14:6).

## Anchor Text

81

"The body is a unit, though it is made up of many parts; and though all its parts are many, they form one body. So it is with Christ. For we were all baptized by one Spirit into one body—whether Jews or Greeks, slave or free—and we were all given the one Spirit to drink" (1 Corinthians 12:12, 13).

## WRITER ACKNOWLEDGMENT OF RESOURCES

Mead, Frank S., revised by Samuel S. Hill. *Handbook of Denominations*. Nashville, Tenn.: Abingdon Press, 1985.

Ministerial Association of the General Conference of Seventh-day Adventists. *Seventh-day Adventists Believe*. Hagerstown, Md.: Review and Herald Publishing Association, 1988.

Neusner, Jacob, ed. *World Religions in America*. Louisville, Ky.: Westminster/John Knox Press, 1994.

## Bible Search

1. In 1 Corinthians 12 Paul writes about the diversity of gifts and the unity of spirit that should exist within the body of Christ, His church. We can conclude, therefore, that what Paul says in this chapter also applies to the Protestant churches of today. Read the entire chapter and answer the following questions.

   A. According to verses 1-3, what important confession binds all Christians together into one faith?

   B. Read verses 4-11. From what Paul says about the different kinds of spiritual gifts, what admonition can be applied to Protestant churches?

# Reaction

## Discussion Questions

1. When sharing your faith with others, why is it helpful to know what they believe?

2. Do you see the Seventh-day Adventist Church as mainline Protestant, evangelical, or fundamentalist? Defend your answer.

3. What do you see as the strengths and the dangers of the social gospel?

4. How politically active should Protestant churches become when dealing with social issues?

5. Do you think it would be a good idea for the Seventh-day Adventist Church to have a church creed? Explain.

6. Do you think there will be a union of Protestantism and Catholicism in the future? What circumstances would bring about such a union?

7. Do you think that the "prosperity gospel" is a biblical concept? Defend your answer.

C. As you read verses 12-26, list at least two guidelines that should be heeded by Protestant Christians today.

D. According to verses 27-31, what concluding suggestion does Paul make that still holds true today? What are the greater gifts? (See chapter 13:1-3, 13.)

2. There are various ways that the unity of believers can be expressed and made evident. Read and summarize the following texts that deal with Christian unity.

A. 2 Corinthians 13:11.

B. Ephesians 4: 13.

C. John 13:34, 35.

D. Galatians 5:24, 25.

E. Galatians 3:28.

## Personal Response

Today we find a serious lack of unity between every major segment of society. What can you do to bring greater spiritual harmony into your home, your school, among your friends, or in your personal life? Since relationships between people mirror the relationship they have with Jesus Christ, how can you be more open and receptive to God's love for you?

## Practical Application

1. Some Christians believe that the unity of Catholicism is evidence of spiritual strength, while the many denominations within Protestantism is a sign of spiritual disarray and weakness. Interview five to eight adults and ask them whether they agree or disagree with the statement and to defend their answer. You may wish to work with another student and have the interviews videotaped. Combine their responses with your personal convictions on the tape or write your report to be shared with the class.

2. Divide into groups of three or four students and develop and present a skit that illustrates a belief or the worship liturgy of one of the denominations mentioned in this lesson.

3. Attend a Quaker, Mennonite, Baptist, or Pentecostal church service and interview one teenager and one adult. Write a 350-word report and be prepared to share it with the class. If attendance at a worship service is not possible, conduct personal interviews with at least two people who are members of the church.

4. Read *The Great Controversy*, page 588:1-3. Write a 300-word paper, summarizing what you read and expressing your reactions to your reading.

Religion is not a way of looking at certain things.
It is a certain way of looking at everything.

# Lesson 9

# A World That Worships

In his book *Alien Gods On American Turf*, Terry Muck writes about the increasing possibility of people living next door, working where you do, or attending your school who are ethnically, culturally, or religiously different from you. In the chapter "New Neighbors," the author cites a friendship that developed between Molly, a Christian high-school student, and Balu, a practicing Hindu.

Both Molly and Balu were on the school's debate team, and the first thing Molly discovered about Balu's religion was how it affected his behavior. He ate a vegetarian diet, had high moral standards, which included no drinking of alcoholic beverages or sex outside of marriage, and had a high respect for her religion. She was surprised that he was doing a better job of living a good, clean life than many of the Christians she knew. But then there were some things that she didn't like. There were a large number of statues and images in Balu's house, and where many students hang memorabilia from their car's rearview mirror, Balu hung a small image of a Hindu deity. In some ways his life was similar to hers, but in other ways, it was very different.

Molly found her friendship with Balu a very positive experience. When at times they talked about God and the meaning of life, his explanations challenged Molly to think seriously about what she believed. It was different from talking with her Christian friends with whom she generally agreed. One discussion that particularly stood out in Molly's mind was the time their debate team was having some serious problems. Molly confided in Balu, "I just don't know what to do."

"You're a Christian, right?" he said. Molly affirmed that she was. "Christians pray, don't they?" Balu questioned. Molly also acknowledged that was true. "OK then; so pray," was Balu's straightforward reply.

To her surprise, Molly discovered that in some ways Balu was of greater help to her than her Christian friends.[1] She began to wonder what her responsibility was to people who believed so differently from the way she did. Was it necessary for her to talk about her faith in Jesus Christ and her Christian beliefs, or was she just supposed to be a good friend and let her actions speak for themselves? Was her primary task to share Christ with Balu or simply help Balu to be the best Hindu he could be?

**The Need to Know**

Ours is a world of great religious diversity in matters of worship, celebration, and everyday customs. With the acceleration of worldwide communication and travel, our planet has been rapidly reduced to a "global village." It has become commonplace to rub shoulders with people of non-Christian religions. It's important, therefore, to have a basic understanding of the world's religions that will enable us to respect other points of view as well as intelligently dialogue and effectively communicate our faith with others.

In our brief overview of some of the world's major religions, you will discover that they generally fall into two basic categories: Western and Eastern religions. Western religions—Judaism, Christianity, and Islam—are generally characterized as religions of **divine revelation**, religion based on man's response to special revelation from God. Eastern religions, such as Hinduism, Buddhism, and Taoism, are religions of **human realization**, religion focused on humanity's endeavor to discover the divine.

Although there are many more world religions than those mentioned above, our focus will be on these six because of their increasingly significant impact upon today's world. In our survey we will take a look at the world's religions in the context of their historical development, and for that reason our study will begin with the most ancient forms of spirituality.

**Evolution or Devolution**

There are opposing views as to the kind of spirituality that existed at the dawn of human civilization and its relationship to today's world religions. Evolutionists advance the idea that the earliest form of human spirituality was a primitive religion known as *Animism*, the "mother-religion"

from which all other religions evolved. Animism was based on a primitive view of reality, that some kind of spirit animated all of nature, leading to the belief of souls, ghosts, and spirits. It was believed that these entities manifested themselves through some kind of energy that permeated the forces of nature and exercised control over their lives. The fear of offending the spirits created a desire to communicate with them and initiated the practice of ancestor worship and human sacrifice. Gradually some of the spirits received the rank of powerful deities, out of which polytheism emerged. Evolutionists also claim that as civilizations advanced, the idea of a supreme ruler replaced the notion of many local chiefs. In like fashion, religion moved from the idea of many gods to one supreme god, giving rise to monotheism.

The Bible teaches the very opposite of the evolutionary view of history. God's Word declares that humankind's initial act of devotion toward the Creator was based on God's original revelation to Adam and Eve. Even after Adam and Eve's fall, the basic truths about God and the way of redemption were handed down by the patriarchs for thousands of years. For those who rejected these divinely revealed truths, there occurred a devolution (deterioration) of religion that eventually led to animism, polytheism, and nature worship. These became the core element in the ancient religions of Egypt, Babylon, Mesopotamia, Greece, and Rome, with their elaborate system of gods and goddesses.

The Bible states that "[humankind] exchanged the truth of God for a lie, and worshiped and served created things rather than the Creator" (Romans 1:25). While the errors associated with animism eventually became the spiritual heart and soul of a worldwide array of emerging heathen religions, there were those who did not barter away the truth for falsehood. Many of the sacred truths preserved by the patriarchs from Adam to Abraham became part of the Jewish canon (Old Testament), which, in turn, became the basic foundation of the Christian Scripture. These divinely inspired truths stand in stark contrast to the ancient folklore and spiritual myths of paganism and non-Christian religions.

## JUDAISM: PROCLAIMING YAHWEH

Judaism had its origin when Abraham received God's call to leave the idolatrous region of Ur in Babylonia and go to the land of Canaan (Genesis 12:1-3). It was not until the Exodus from Egypt over 400 years later that the Jews were formally organized into a "holy nation," a people with a divine mandate: "You are my witnesses . . . that I am God" (Isaiah 43:12). "I will also make you a light for the Gentiles, that you may bring my salvation to the ends of the earth" (Isaiah 49:6). History is crucial to the Jews, for in their past God spoke to them through the prophets, establishing a covenant relationship with them.

Although the Jewish people received from God the redemptive truths that became known as the Old Testament, they failed to grasp their real significance and consequently failed to enlighten the world regarding the coming of the Messiah and

the nature of His mission. Following their rejection of Christ as the Messiah and the stoning of Stephen, the city of Jerusalem was destroyed and the nation taken into captivity by the Romans in A.D. 70. These events signaled the transition from ancient Judaism to modern Judaism—from a closely knit people focused on temple sacrifices and priests to a scattered people whose fading heritage is kept alive by synagogue rituals and rabbis. Although Christianity traces its roots to ancient Judaism, we will focus on modern Judaism, the Judaism you and I see in today's world.

### Sacred Writings

The sacred writings of Judaism are the *Torah* and the *Talmud*. The Torah has reference to the Old Testament, but Jews do not hold each part of their Scripture with equal importance. The **Law** (the first five books)

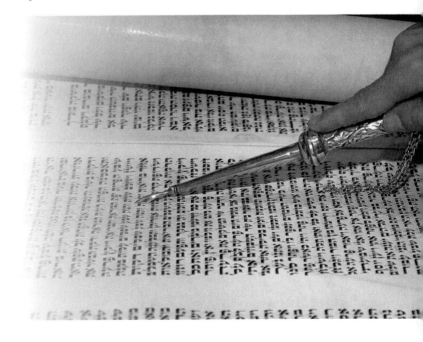

is the most important, followed by the **Prophets** (Isaiah, Jeremiah, Ezekiel, etc.) and then the **Writings** (Psalms, Proverbs, Job, etc.). The Talmud is a vast collection of oral traditions, stories, commentaries, and authoritative opinions on the Torah. More than 2,000 scholars and rabbis worked from around A.D. 250-600 to compile the Talmud—the English edition filling thirty-six volumes with over 36,000 pages.[2] Though life is to be lived in Judaism according to the teachings of the Torah, the foundation of modern Judaism—its basic understanding of the Torah—is the Talmud.

### Jewish Worship

The home and the synagogue are primarily responsible for the worship experiences, spiritual unity, and moral training within Judaism. The seventh-day Sabbath is a time of family togetherness, prayer, and devotions, as well as formal worship in the synagogue conducted by the rabbi. The formal ceremony denoting a thirteen-year-old boy's arrival into manhood, and with it the adherence to the 613 commandments of Judaism, is known as *bar mitzvah*. Though not as commonly practiced, the ceremony for girls is called *bat mitzvah*. Regarding education, most Jews send their children to public schools rather than Jewish parochial schools.

Much of Jewish worship involves active participation in daily, weekly, and yearly ceremonies and holy days. In calling attention to significant historical events, these prescribed rituals provide Jews the opportunity to renew their faith and commitment to God. The following are the yearly festivals:

*Passover:* This feast, along with its primary meal the *Seder,* commemorates one of the most important events in Jewish history— the deliverance of Israel from Egyptian slavery. *Shabuot:* This festival, known as Pentecost within Christianity, celebrates the giving of the Ten Commandments at Mount Sinai. *Purim:* This is a memorial of Queen Esther's heroic act of saving the Jews in Persia from Haman's death decree. *Rosh Hashanah:* This is the Jewish New Year, observed on the first two days of the month of Tishai (September–October). *Yom Kippur:* This is the holiest day of the Jewish year, the Day of Atonement. No food or drink is consumed during this day; it is a day devoted to confession of sins and reconciliation with God. *Hanukkah:* This is the only yearly festival that has no biblical basis. It celebrates the heroism of the Maccabees in 165 B.C. against the Syrian oppressors. Since Hanukkah occurs near Christmas time, the Jews have turned this festival into a time of gift giving, making it one of the more popular holidays within Judaism.

### Divisions Within Judaism

*Orthodox Judaism:* Around 10 percent of American Jews are members of Orthodox synagogues where the Torah is accepted as the exact words of God. Orthodox Jews are extremely loyal to tradition and emphasize strict observance of the Torah as interpreted by the rabbis. Some Orthodox groups choose to live a life that in many ways separates them from everybody else: they speak a Jewish language called Yiddish, pray entirely in Hebrew, wear distinctly Jewish attire, observe rigid dietary laws, and generally do not eat, live, or socialize with Gentiles.

*Reform Judaism:* About 35 percent of Jews in the United States agree to a liberal kind of Judaism that seeks to modernize outmoded customs and practices of the past. Though this branch of Judaism affirms that the Torah is holy, it observes only those laws and ceremonies that are compatible to the culture and lifestyle of modern society. Reform Jews tend to disregard dietary laws, while eating, and mingling with Gentiles is generally encouraged. They may attend synagogue services on the Sabbath but have abandoned many of the traditional practices concerning Sabbath observance. Reform Jews drive to their place of worship, in contrast to Orthodox Jews, who attempt to live within walking distance of the synagogue. There is little consensus regarding doctrinal beliefs in Reform Judaism.

*Conservative Judaism:* It is estimated that around 45 percent of American Jews belong to Conservative Judaism, which arose during the nineteenth century as an attempt to find a middle ground between the Orthodox and Reform branches. To the Conservative, Judaism is not static but a growing, widening faith of a people who are absorbing the influences of other cultures, yet retaining their own ethnic and religious customs.

## Judaism Summary

Judaism is primarily a religion of **deed**, rather than **creed**. Though monotheism is a foundational belief, the idea of individual salvation and a heavenly existence is not prominent in Judaism. While acknowledging sin as the breaking of God's law, there is no concept of saving grace or substitionary atonement as in Christianity. Salvation is attained by penitence, prayer, and good works. The idea of the coming of a personal Messiah has been abandoned in favor of a Messianic age characterized by truth, justice, and freedom of oppression. Consequently, the primary concern of modern Judaism is not preparing for the hereafter, but rather, working for peace, prosperity, and social justice here and now. Such a spiritual outlook led to the creation of Zionism in 1895, a movement dedicated to restoring the Jewish people to the land of Israel. In recent times it has become a unifying factor within American Judaism.

## HINDUISM: ENCOMPASSING ALL

Hinduism is not only one of the oldest religions known to humankind, it is also one of the most complex. It has no human founder and no datable beginning; it simply emerged out of the primitive religions that preceded it. Modern Hinduism is very much a synthesis of the world's religions—always changing, always accommodating the beliefs and practices of other spiritual systems. For this reason Hinduism can be seen more as a **culture** than a **creed**. Hinduism's tolerance of almost all religious viewpoints is based on the pantheistic concept that all things are bound together by a common "oneness." The vast majority of Hindus—some 700 million—live in India, where they account for over 80 percent of the population. Our study of Hinduism will focus on how it is practiced in that part of the world.

## Sacred Writings

The Hindu scriptures include a massive number of writings that were written over a period of 2,000 years (1400 B.C.–A.D. 500) that reflect the practices and beliefs that arose during that lengthy time period. The *Vedas* are the oldest of the Hindu scriptures, containing hymns of praise, ceremonial instructions, and religious teachings. It is the *Bhagavad-Gita*, however, that is the most sacred, the best known, the most beloved and read of all Hindu works in the entire world.

## Hindu Beliefs

Hinduism is based on the pantheistic concept of the unity of all things, that everything has a common divine essence. This universal divine consciousness is called *Brahman*, an impersonal life force that is beyond all physical and moral distinctions. Since Hindus view Brahman as the ultimate reality from which emanated the entire universe, they see their personal souls *(atman)* as having the same essence as the universal soul (Brahman).

According to Hinduism, humanity's basic problem is its ignorance of man's divine nature. We have somehow forgotten about our oneness with Brahman and are therefore subject to the whims and wishes of our own misguided egos. Since Hindus believe that everything that exists is essentially divine, to believe otherwise is to be in a state of delusion or *maya*. To break away from this illusory state and recognize our oneness with the Divine is what the religion of Hinduism is all about.

Escaping maya is referred to as *moksha* and can either be accomplished by good works, devotion, or mystical experiences carried out over thousands of lifetimes. Such a belief requires the idea of reincarnation—the idea of a continual cycle of rebirths until the soul ultimately dissolves into a blissful oneness with the Divine called *enlightenment* or *god-consciousness*. This embodies the Hindu concept of salvation.

Hinduism views the human race as being deceived by our minds—the place where all critical distinctions are formulated. The remedy proposed is an **altered state**, a **self-induced** trance in which all distinctions seemingly disappear and dissolve into one. An altered state involves Hindu meditation (known as *transcendental meditation*) that is generally induced by various forms of yoga, chanting, fasting, or the use of drugs. While these activities are designed to empty the mind—to terminate the thinking processes and activate a hallucinatory trancelike state, it can also give demonic spirits the opportunity to enter and control the unguarded mind.

As already stated, Hindus teach that humankind, in its normal consciousness, has an illusory view of reality. This means that people mistakenly believe that they are merely human and that they will eventually die. Hinduism maintains that those who believe such errors must experience reincarnation *(samsara)* and learn in future lives what they failed to perceive during this lifetime. The condition into which a person is born in each succeeding life is determined by *karma*. This refers to the law of cause and effect, meaning that each person gets what he or she justly deserves. A person's karma determines the kind of body—whether human, animal, or insect—he or she will receive in the next life. The goal is to achieve enough good karma so that one can escape from the cycle of rebirths and attain divine oneness—enlightenment.

All creatures, man and beast, are thought to be in their present situations because of what they did in previous lives. Karma permits one to blame everything on a previous lifetime, and it cannot be interfered with since it is viewed as a flawless universal process. The tragic impact of such a belief has led not only to centuries of shunning the poor and sick, believing that that's what they deserve, but justifying the cruel inequities of India's *caste system*.

### Hindu Worship

Hinduism believes in one divine essence, yet it worships millions of lesser gods and goddesses. The most well-known deities are Brahma, the creator; Vishnu, the preserver; and Shiva, the destroyer. *Avatars* are gods that have taken human form, and Hindus believe that Vishnu appeared on earth as Krishna, the most popular god in India today. The worship of a deity can take place at home or in a Hindu temple. Performing acts of worship *(puja)* is one way the worshiper can build up good karma. Hindus believe that one can also acquire spiritual "points" through fasting, bathing, chanting, fulfilling vows, dancing, and making contact with holy objects, persons, and places.

According to Hindu scripture, cows, monkeys, rats, and snakes are to be revered as holy and worshiped. Benares (now called Varanasi) is one of India's holiest cities, a city containing some 1,500 temples and bathing places, and housing over half a million images of Hindu gods and goddesses. The city is located on the Ganges River, and it is believed that bathing in and drinking its holy water cleanses the soul and cures diseases. Holy men, such as *gurus* (spiritual teachers) are highly revered, and in serving them, Hindus hope that some of their holiness will rub off on them.

### Hinduism Summary

From a Christian perspective, Hinduism is a religion of escape rather than fulfillment. It is a system of spirituality based entirely on human endeavor. It is the belief that each person has many lifetimes to gain salvation through good works and the worship of millions of gods and goddesses. Hinduism **affirms** that all religions are equally valid pathways to God and salvation and **denies** Christianity's claim that salvation is a gift of God that is received only through Jesus Christ. Our Hindu friends need to hear the good news that it is not **innumerable** lifetimes of extreme devotion and good works that bring salvation, but it is simply believing in that **One** sinless life that has already lived and died in their behalf.

### Anchor Text

"Since we are God's offspring, we should not think that the divine being is like gold or silver or stone—an image made by man's design and skill. In the past God overlooked such ignorance, but now he commands all people everywhere to repent" (Acts 17:29, 30).

### NOTES

1. Terry Muck, *Alien Gods On American Turf* (Wheaton, Ill.: Victor Books, 1990), pages 21-23.

2. Herbert Lockyer, Sr., ed., *Nelson's Illustrated Bible Dictionary* (Nashville, Tenn.: Thomas Nelson, Inc. 1986), pages 1028, 1029.

### WRITER ACKNOWLEDGMENT OF RESOURCES

Braswell, George W. Jr. *Understanding World Religions.* Nashville, Tenn.: Broadman Press, 1983.

Burke, T. Patrick. *Introduction to the Major Religions.* Cambridge, Mass.: Blackwell Publishers, Inc., 1996.

Halverson, Dean C., ed. *The Compact Guide to World Religions.* Minneapolis, Minn.: Bethany House Publishers, 1996.

## Bible Search

1. The decisive difference between ancient Judaism and modern Judaism hinges on their view of Jesus Christ, the Messiah. Whereas God's purpose for ancient Judaism was to make known to the world the saving work of the coming Messiah, modern Judaism denies that He came or

# Reaction

## Discussion Questions

1. What are the advantages and disadvantages of having a non-Christian for a close friend?

2. Why have all major civilizations chosen to believe heathen religions and worship pagan gods?

3. What do you see as the greatest strength and the greatest weakness of modern Judaism?

4. How would you go about convincing a Hindu of the dangers of an altered state of consciousness?

5. What are the major differences between resurrection and reincarnation?

6. Why do you think India has for so many centuries clung to Hindu beliefs and practices?

7. What problems can arise when a person reads the New Testament and does not make a distinction between "spiritual" and "literal" Jews? (As an example, see Revelation 7:1-8.)

## Personal Response

Ancient religions are often characterized by a wide variety of rituals and ceremonies. Apart from Christ these acts of devotion have very little, if any, redemptive value. Do you find yourself participating in a lot of religious activities without having Jesus Christ as the primary focus? In your relationship with others, does your life deny or affirm that Jesus is your Savior and Lord?

that His redemptive work is needed by the world. Read the following New Testament texts and summarize what each passage says regarding this significant transition.
A. Matthew 21:33-46.
B. Matthew 23:13, 37, 38.
C. Acts 2:36-39.

2. When the Jewish people, through their leaders, rejected Jesus, they **ceased** to exist as God's chosen people, although they **continued** their struggle to survive as a political nation. In light of this, the New Testament makes a clear-cut distinction between "spiritual" Jews, or Israel (those who believe in Jesus), and the "literal" Jews, who today constitute modern Judaism. Read the following passages from the New Testament and summarize what Paul said regarding this important **biblical** distinction.
A. Romans 2:28, 29
B. Galatians 2:15, 16.
C. Galatians 3:26-29.

3. The lesson states that when Hindus engage in activities that are designed to "empty the mind," it gives "demonic spirits an opportunity to seize and control the unguarded mind." Read Matthew 12:43-45 and explain how Christ's statement relates to this Hindu practice.

## Practical Application

1. In the opening story of Molly and Balu, two questions conclude the story. Write a 100-word response to these questions.

2. Attend a Jewish synagogue on Friday night or on Sabbath with another person. Your report describing the synagogue, the worship service, and your interview with the rabbi or a synagogue member should be written as a question-and-answer dialogue between the two of you that can be presented to the class.

3. You are a member of a public forum comprised of three people—a representative of Hinduism, of Judaism, and of Christianity. You are Christianity's representative, and you have just been asked this question: As a Christian you claim that salvation comes only through Jesus Christ. However, Hinduism and Judaism were in existence over a thousand years before Christianity even existed. Were not people saved through other religions before the time of Christianity? Write your response to this question.

The heart of the human problem is the problem of the human heart.

# Lesson 10

## The East Invades the West

An invasion is an attack designed to defeat and destroy the enemy! Fortunately, most of us have never been the victims of an invasion—or have we? An invasion, you know, doesn't have to be a military attack. Houses are often invaded by all kinds of creeping things, our bodies can be invaded by germs or deadly viruses, while a society can be attacked and overthrown by political ideas or religious beliefs. Remember that old adage "The pen is mightier than the sword"? There is a spiritual warfare going on today as the East increasingly bombards the West with new and unusual ways to think, live, and worship. For example, reincarnation, acupuncture, yoga, the martial arts, as well as numerous New Age ideas and Eastern health practices have become household concepts in today's world. In this spiritual warfare between contrasting beliefs and practices, can you discern truth from error?

As you study Islam, Buddhism, and Taoism in this lesson, you will become aware of some of the similarities and differences between the religions of the West and the East, as well as noting their positive and negative qualities.

### ISLAM: AN UNCOMPROMISING CALL

Islam is the world's fastest growing religion, making up 20 percent of the world's population. It has become the second-largest religion, second only to Christianity. Islam is a Western religion, though it has some cultural and theological features that are Eastern. This stems back to its beginning when its founder, Mohammed, in the seventh century A.D., combined elements from Judaism, Christianity, and paganism (Arabian religions) when establishing Islam.

### Islam: Its Beginning

Mohammed grew up in Mecca, near the western coastline of Saudi Arabia, which was a religious center for the worship of a host of pagan deities. Influenced by some Jews and Christians who lived in the area, Mohammed began to denounce idolatry and declared that only *Allah* ("the God" in Arabic) was to be worshiped. In A.D. 610, at the age of forty, Mohammed began receiving visions, as well as spoken revelations from the angel Gabriel. These revelations were eventually compiled into Islam's sacred scripture, the Qur'an (formerly spelled Koran), meaning "recitations." Mohammed's opposition to all forms of idol worship forced him to flee to Yathrib in A.D. 622, a town located about 200 miles north and later renamed Medina. His escape is called the Hegira (*Hijrah*, or "flight"), which Muslims view as the official beginning of Islam as well as their religious calendar. The year

of Mohammed's death in A.D. 632, for example, is listed as 10 AH ("in the year of the Hegira").

Before his death Mohammed organized an Islamic theocracy, enabling Muslims to govern and conquer in the name of Allah so that within one century, they ruled over an area greater than the Roman Empire at its height. Islam was very effective in leading the Arab world out of the darkness of pagan idolatry into the truth of One Almighty God. Islam has continued as a powerful, worldwide force since its beginning nearly 1,400 years ago.

In the book *THE 100: A Ranking of the Most Influential Persons in History*, Mohammed is ranked number one. In defending his choice of ranking Mohammed over Jesus, who is ranked third, the author states that though Jesus presented some of the most remarkable teachings ever given to humankind, "they are not widely followed. In fact, they are not even generally accepted. . . . The injunction to 'Love your enemy,' . . . remains an intriguing but basically untried suggestion."[1] What a sad commentary regarding the followers of Jesus!

### Beliefs and Obligations

The term *Islam* means "submission" to the will of Allah, and *Muslim* means "one who submits." Islam can be divided into beliefs *(inman)* and obligations *(deen)*. These are the **basic beliefs** of Islam:

**1. Monotheism.** Islam holds that Allah is one and emphatically rejects the idea of the Trinity. Emphasis on Allah's transcendence makes him practically unreachable and unknowable to his followers. Allah's presence in the world is not seen through supernatural signs but in the orderliness of nature and in the miraculous giving of the Qur'an.

**2. Prophets.** Islam holds that Allah has sent prophets to the nations, such as Noah, Abraham, Moses, John the Baptist, and Jesus. The Qur'an says this about Jesus: "They [the Jews] did not kill him, nor did they crucify him, but they thought they did"[2] (Sura IV:156). Though they view Him as a prophet, Muslims reject the notion that Jesus was the Son of God, insisting that God would never subject Himself to mockery and death. Each prophet was given for a particular age, with Mohammed being the last and greatest of all prophets.

**3. Scripture.** Muslims believe in many inspired books, such as the Jewish Torah (books of Moses), the Psalms, and the Gospels. They contend, however, that only the Qur'an in the Arabic language is the perfect expression of Allah's will. It alone has been preserved from alterations and corruption and thus supersedes all earlier revelations. The Qur'an is about four-fifths the length of the New Testament and has often been referred to as the most memorized book in the world.

**4. Angels.** Muslims believe in the existence of intermediary beings called angels. The highest angel is Gabriel, and those at the bottom of the hierarchy are fallen angels, the *jinn*, from which we get the word *genie*. The primary work of angels is to record the good and bad deeds of every person.

**5. Judgment.** The Qur'an teaches that every person must stand before Allah in judgment. Those whose good deeds outweigh their bad deeds will enter paradise, and those whose bad deeds outweigh their good deeds will be condemned to hell.

**6. Salvation.** The Qur'an rejects the idea of divine atonement and redemption; salvation depends solely on human merit. For the Muslim, salvation is not based on God's **grace**, but rather, on man's acceptance of God's **guidance** in accomplishing good works. Islam upholds an uncompromising position as to its beliefs, worship, and lifestyle, emphasizing prescribed rituals rather than a personal relationship with God.

These are the primary **obligations** of Islam: (1) **Recitation.** A Muslim must recite the Shahadah, meaning "to bear witness," which is audibly affirming that "there is no God but Allah, and Mohammed is his messenger." Saying the Shahadah publicly and with conviction is all it takes to become a Muslim. (2) **Prayer.** The practice of prayer *(salat)* is required of all Muslims five times a day—at dawn, noon, midafternoon, dusk, and before retiring. They must wash themselves in a prescribed way before praying and pray facing Mecca. In countries where Islam is the state religion, the call to prayer is sounded by the *muezzin* (a Muslim crier) from a tower called a *minaret*, which is part of the *mosque*, the place of worship. Islam's holy day is Friday, when believers are expected to gather at the mosque for a noon prayer and sermon. (3) **Alms.** The giving of alms *(zakat)* is required of all Muslims, which involves the giving of 2.5 percent of their income to the poor and needy.

(4) **Fasting** *(sawm).* In commemoration of Mohammed's receiving the Qur'an in the month of Ramadan, Muslims are to refrain from eating or drinking anything in the daylight hours during the entire month.

(5) **Pilgrimage.** All Muslims are required, if at all possible, to make a pilgrimage *(Hajj)* to Mecca at least once in their lifetime. All must wear a white garment *(ihram)* to demonstrate their equality before Allah. Lengthy and complex ceremonies and rituals are performed for about two weeks, most of them centering around the *Kaaba* (a Meccan shrine containing a black stone on which Abraham was to have supposedly carried out the sacrifice of Ishmael). (6) **Holy War.** In addition to the five main pillars of the faith, there is a sixth—the holy war *(Jihad).* Holy wars are those that are fought defending the Islamic faith and community, and anyone who dies in such a conflict is promised immediate entrance into paradise.

## Islamic Divisions

Ever since the seventh century, Islam has been divided between the *Sunni* and the *Shiite* over the issue of a successor to Mohammed. Today the Sunni, which make up nearly 80 percent of the world's Muslim population, continue to maintain that there should be a separation between civil and religious authorities, while the Shiites hold that the Islamic leaders should exercise both political and religious power. Other significant Islamic groups in the United States are the *Sufii* and the *Nation of Islam.*

The Nation of Islam, the most prominent organization within the Black Muslim movement, is more of a social protest against traditional White American culture than it is a religious movement. Many young African-Americans are attracted to the Nation of Islam because of its strong emphasis against drugs and sexual immorality; the rehabilitation of convicts, drug addicts, and alcoholics; and its very aggressive approach to gangs and gang violence. Additionally, they are attracted to the fundamental belief that African-Americans should become economically self-sufficient, avoiding reliance upon government welfare and white-owned businesses.

Generally speaking, the Nation of Islam is often viewed as a contradictory blend of Islamic and Christian beliefs. Its members tend to abide by a strict Islamic code of behavior regarding such things as diet, dress, and interpersonal relations. Orthodox Islam declares, however, that the racism of the Nation of Islam—its present emphasis on Black supremacy and separatism, white conspiracies to destroy black people, the inherent wickedness of the white race, and the Jews as a special enemy—all contradict the basic tenor of Islam as a truly interracial religion. On the other side, the Nation of Islam also undermines people's faith in Christianity and the Bible. Its leadership has often declared that the Bible was used to enslave Black people and that the White man's heaven is the Black man's hell. The Nation of Islam challenges Christianity on every major belief: the nature of God, the validity of the Bible, the way of salvation, the person and work of Jesus, and the nature of life after death. In dealing with the problems of racial tensions and inequities, its language of blame and revenge is likewise contrary to the spirit of Christ.

## BUDDHISM: DENYING SELF

Buddhism began as a reform movement within Hinduism in the sixth century B.C., about the time the Jews were in captivity in Babylon. Its founder was Siddhartha Gautama, the son of an extremely wealthy *rajah* (prince). Though surrounded by extravagant luxury, he became profoundly dissatisfied with life as he observed the people around him suffering and dying from poverty and disease. Gautama was convinced that Hinduism had become corrupt and the leadership ineffective in dealing with the plight of the common people. At the age of twenty-nine, he left his wife, an infant son, and a lavish lifestyle and wholeheartedly devoted himself to his quest for ultimate truth and enlightenment. For several years he attempted to find the answers to the ills of human existence through the mastery of ancient wisdom and self-mortification. Eventually he gave up extreme asceticism in favor of meditation and solitude, later referred to as the "Middle Path"—a pathway between pleasure-seeking and self-torture. In a peak moment during days of deep reflection while sitting under a bodhi tree, he became convinced he had found **the** solution and that he was now a "*Buddha*," a title meaning "one who is awake," or the "enlightened one." For the remaining forty-five years of his life, he traveled throughout northern India, sharing his beliefs with anyone who was willing to listen. At the time of his death, Buddha had thousands of followers.

### Basic Beliefs

A primary teaching of Buddha is the *Four Noble Truths:* First, human life is full of suffering; second, the cause of suffering is human desire and passion; third, eliminate all human desire and you will eliminate suffering; fourth, desire can be eliminated by following the "Eightfold Path," a highly regimented program that emphasizes right beliefs, right morals, and right discipline, interwoven with a series of meditative practices. The goal is to eliminate the cause of suffering by achieving a state of consciousness in which one progressively disdains the yearnings of self and denies the existence of a personal identity. The trancelike condition in which all human desires and cravings are extinguished is called *nirvana*, a term that literally means "blowing out" the flame of desire. Buddhism's ultimate goal of enlightenment—liberation from *samsara* (cycle of rebirths) and release from the deceptive (illusory) experiences of human life—is attained through a ritualistic closure of the self.

### Basic Divisions

Over the course of time, Buddhism split into two major divisions, which, in turn, subdivided into scores of sects. The primary issue is how enlightenment is attained and whether it is accessible to everyone or only a few. Those who say enlightenment is available to all are called *Mahayana*, and those who maintain that enlightenment is only available for a committed few (the monks) are called *Theravada.* Mahayana Buddhists see the Buddha as one to whom they can pray for grace and deliverance. They also believe in celestial beings called *bodisattvas* who, through many lifetimes, have built up a reservoir of karmic merit that can be shared with struggling Buddhists who need help. In contrast, Theravada Buddhists see the Buddha as merely a human ideal and that enlightenment is attained solely through one's own efforts.

Buddhists do not believe in the existence of God, and this has a definite impact on what takes place in the Buddhist temple. The common worshipers bring their offerings of food, wine, and incense to honor the Buddha, to pay homage to the scores of images of the gods of Buddhist folklore, and to appease the spirits of deceased ancestors. Buddhists generally believe that bringing offerings is all that is required of them and that the priests will do the more difficult obligations for them.

**Buddhist Monks**

Buddha taught that the ideal life was that of a monk. The cloistered life within the monastery provides the best opportunity to achieve enlightenment because only monks have the time to complete all requirements of the Eightfold Path. While monks gain good karma by renouncing the world, the lay people gain good karma by supplying their needs. A monk's belongings are simple: three robes, one belt, one bowl, one needle, and one water strainer. Monks generally observe some 227 rules, which include the wearing of special-colored robes, having shaven heads, reciting vows, chanting and meditating, begging for food, and straining all drinking water so as not to take the life of any animal forms. It's ironic that while monks are taught to respect the tiniest life forms, at the same time, they are trained to renounce their own lives.

**Zen Buddhism**

*Zen,* which means "meditation," has become the most popular form of Buddhism in the West, with scores of *zendos* (Zen centers) springing up throughout North America. It is a kind of Buddhism in which enlightenment is totally dependent upon self-effort—highly disciplined meditation. The objective is to push one's mental faculties into a **nonthinking** mode by meditating upon a *koan*—a phrase, question, or problem that is insoluble to the intellect. The rock group Nirvana and the title of their album *Nevermind* reflect this Buddhist idea of human mindlessness. Zen's goal is *satori* (nirvana), the cessation of all rational thought, desires, and passions, and with it the cancellation of one's individual identity. Zen has become so popular because it promotes detachment from anything that causes pain, stress, or anxiety. It has no transcendent God to worship and obey, no binding scriptures to follow, and little concern about one's soul or the afterlife. Without a belief in God or reliance upon a divine Savior and an ultimate Authority, the Zen Buddhist simply looks inward for spiritual awareness, peace of mind, liberation, and earthly fulfillment.

## TAOISM: GOING WITH THE FLOW

The mystical concepts of Taoism (pronounced Dowism) are important to understand because they lie at the heart of many Asian cultures and religions. The founder of Taoism is a legendary Chinese figure of the sixth century B.C. by the name of Lao Tzu. In his book, *Tao Te Ching*, Lao Tzu expounded his belief that true harmony could exist only where people lived according to the **internal** laws of nature rather than the imposed **external** laws of society.

According to Taoism, the key to spiritual harmony is the *Tao*, an extremely complex concept that is often translated the "way," or the "path,"—an eternal principle, an ultimate reality, a creative, underlying **force** that flows through nature and governs the cosmos. To live in harmony with the Tao is to be in tune with the universe, to flow with the natural order of things. The primary quality of Taoism is nonresistance—taking no unnatural action, shunning aggressiveness, and simply letting nature, the Tao, take its course. Humankind must live passively, avoiding all forms of stress and violence, and simply align itself with the forces of nature. Going the way the Tao flows will naturally lead to harmony, health, and peace. This unexplainable flow of vital energy, known as—*Chi, Ki,* or *Prana,* is uti-

lized by skilled practitioners for spiritual purification, to attain astonishing physical powers, and hopefully to gain immortality.

Taoism's emphasis of ignoring or withdrawing from pain, difficulties, and the ills of society can discourage scientific inquiry, belittle human initiative, and lead to an attitude of indifference. Taoism was popularized in the United States by the hippie generation whose "tune in, drop out" mentality mirrored the Taoist philosophy.

The Tao consists of the *Yin* and the *Yang*, a duality of opposing forces, yet at the same time, balancing and interacting with each other, creating and sustaining all life. Examples of Yang are male, light, life, active, hot, good, and strong. The Yin counterparts are female, darkness, death, passive, cold, evil, and weak. Taoism maintains that they are **coequal** and that we cannot know the one without the contrast of the other. For example, we cannot know the good without the evil to give us perspective. This concept contradicts the Bible, where God strictly forbade Adam and Eve to gain a "the knowledge of good **and** evil," for in so doing, "you will surely die" (Genesis 2:17). In the Bible, evil is always presented as an unnecessary intruder rather than a legitimate coequal with good.

Starting as an ethical philosophy, Taoism eventually developed into a religion that became encumbered with all kinds of superstitious beliefs and practices. Taoism is animistic, pantheistic, and naturalistic, with nature being viewed as the essence and measure of all things. This blend of worldviews led to the worship of all kinds of spirits and communication with the spirit world. Through the centuries, the mystical force of the Tao has opened the door to various occult practices—activities whose mysterious power is "hidden" from human understanding and is "beyond" rational explanation.

## Eastern Religion: Its Impact

During the nineteenth century, America was introduced to Eastern thought by transcendentalists such as Ralph Waldo Emerson and Henry David Thoreau, who were strongly influenced by Hindu philosophy. Events that greatly expanded the influence of Eastern thought in the twentieth century were the influx of Hindu gurus, the cultural revolution of the 1960s and 70s, and the explosion in our day of pantheistic ideas and practices in the media—especially through TV, movies, and music. It's been said that the "theologian" who has had the greatest influence on people's ideas about God in our day is George Lucas, the producer of the *Star Wars* Trilogy. In coining the phrase "May the force be with you," he made the pantheistic view of God as believable and acceptable as the biblical view.

Eastern religions, as well as the New Age movement, have firmly implanted upon America's consciousness the pantheistic idea of a universal life force, a creative energy that pervades the entire cosmos. The Bible teaches us, however, to **reject** any belief or practice that is connected with an altered state or is based on a pantheistic view of God (1 John 4:1, 2). For example:

**Yoga:** From Hinduism comes the idea that universal energy flows from the air we breathe, thus the word *prana*, the Sanskrit word for "breath." It is for this reason that yoga, as practiced by Hindus, emphasizes breathing techniques and exercises that are designed to distribute prana throughout the body. *Yoga* means "to yoke," to create an altered state whereby the individual is mystically yoked with the divine.

**Martial Arts:** We need to carefully assess not only the practical objectives but also the underlying philosophy that undergirds the martial arts. While Aikido, Ninjitsu, and Tai Chi are deeply steeped in Eastern mysticism, Judo, Jujitsu, Karate, and Tae Kwon Do have in Western practice a greater focus on physical self-defense techniques. As the martial arts developed in ancient China and Japan as a form of self-defense, they also became involved in meditation, mind control, and spiritual development associated with a higher consciousness. Perhaps for this reason the practice hall—*dojo* (Japanese), *dojang* (Korean), *kwoon* (Chinese)—where the martial arts are studied is traditionally called "The Place of Enlightenment." Much martial-arts training is designed to achieve oneness with the universal energy, enabling one to utilize Chi, the invisible life force that supposedly flows through all things.

**Acupuncture:** This is only one of many Eastern medical practices that involves the manipulation of vital energy that is said to flow through the human body. Acupuncture is based on Chinese philosophy that defines disease as an imbalance in the flow of energy or is the by-product of an unenlightened consciousness. There is a general consensus among Christian scholars that Eastern practices that utilize the so-called "life force" may often be associated with altered states of consciousness, psychic phenomena, and contact with spirits.

In summary, it can be said that Eastern religions generally interpret God as a universal energy or "life force." Since this is also seen as the sum and substance of humankind, self is viewed as divine and is therefore capable of healing, governing, and saving itself. The philosophy of Eastern religions that everything is divine not only eliminates the need for a saving relationship with a transcendent God, but it also endorses the occult as a viable and easily accessible alternative.

## Anchor Text

"Do not believe every spirit, but test the spirits to see whether they are from God, because many false prophets have gone out into the world. This is how you can recognize the Spirit of God: Every spirit that acknowledges that Jesus Christ has come in the flesh is from God, but every spirit that does not acknowledge Jesus is not from God. This is the spirit of the antichrist, which . . . even now is already in the world" (1 John 4:1-3).

**NOTES**

1. Michael H. Hart, *THE 100: A Ranking of the Most Influential Persons in History* (New York, N.Y.: A & W Publishers, Inc., 1978), pages 50, 51.

2. *The Koran*, translated by N. J. Dawood (New York, N.Y.: Viking Penguin Inc., 1956), page 382.

**WRITER ACKNOWLEDGMENT OF RESOURCES**

Burke, T. Patrick. *The Major Religions.* Cambridge, Mass.: Blackwell Publishers, 1996.

Kyle, Richard. *The Religious Fringe: A History of Alternative Religions in America.* Downers Grove, Ill.: InterVarsity Press, 1993.

## Bible Search

1. A core characteristic of Eastern religions is the de-evaluation of rational thought. What does the Bible say regarding the use of the mind in our relationship with God? What is the role of the mind, God's Word, and His Spirit when judging the validity and value of life's experiences? Read the following texts that deal with this issue and write a brief summary of each.

A. Isaiah 1:18

# Reaction

104

## Discussion Questions

1. What is your response to Christ being ranked third because His teachings have not been "widely followed" or "generally accepted"?

2. How would you answer the Muslim's claim that Mohammed was the last and the greatest of all the prophets?

3. How can the Muslims accept the Gospels as inspired and yet not accept Christ as the Savior of the world?

4. In view of the Islamic beliefs and practices, do you see Islam as a redemptive religion? Explain your answer.

5. What do you see as the most positive and negative features of Islam?

6. What do you see as the main difference between Eastern meditation and Christian meditation?

7. How do you think the Taoist determines right from wrong?

8. What do you see as the spiritual dangers in becoming involved with an Eastern practice?

B.  Isaiah 26:3
C.  Matthew 22:37
D.  Acts 17:2
E.  Romans 12:2
F.  Philippians 4:8
G.  1 Peter 1:13

2. The Anchor Text, 1 John 4:1-3, deals with the necessity of judging **all** "spirit" manifestations in light of the teachings of God's Word. Write a 150-word paper explaining what guidance this text, and those listed below, can give you when passing judgment on the display of power associated with the mysterious energies of Eastern religions.
Matthew 7:22, 23;
2 Thessalonians 2:9-12.

## Personal Response

Islam has very clear-cut obligations that are carried out by the believers. Do you have a clear understanding of the primary obligations of your religion?

Are you willing to be as devoted and faithful in your relationship with Jesus as Muslims are to their religion?

## Practical Application

1. Write a 300-word report, based on research and/or a personal interview with a Muslim, on one or more of the topics listed below. In this project you may wish to work with another student and videotape the interviews.
   A.  Fasting during Ramadan
   B.  Pilgrimage to Mecca
   C.  Prayer five times a day
   D.  Muslim life in America

2. Write a 350-word research paper on the positive and negative aspects of one of the following practices:
   A.  Acupuncture
   B.  Martial arts
   C.  Transcendental meditation
   D.  Yoga

3. Together with several of your friends, visit a Buddhist temple or an Islamic mosque in your area and interview some of the worshipers. You should find out in advance what constitutes appropriate attire and conduct for visitors. An option would be to simply interview people who are Muslim or Buddhist. This report should be 350 words long.

Conscience is like a sundial. When the truth of God
shines on it, it points the right way.

# Lesson 11

## Alternative Religions

Heaven's Gate was a small quasi-religious group of computer programmers that was relatively unknown. But all of this dramatically changed on March 26, 1997, when the media reported the shocking news that thirty-nine of its members had committed mass suicide inside their palatial mansion in Rancho Santa Fe, a ritzy Southern California community near San Diego.

The bizarre details of this tragic event revealed that the theology of Heaven's Gate was a strange mixture of apocalyptic spirituality and sci-fi space travel. The leader of this cultlike group was sixty-six-year-old Marshall Applewhite, a man who claimed to be the reincarnation of Jesus Christ. For about twenty-five years he had vended his ideas about a glorious adventure of riding a spaceship to a better world, where elite believers would reach a higher level of blissful existence. He convinced his followers that their bodies were simply earthly containers for their true, unseen forms, and that these could be released for space travel only by death itself.

The cult members' daily routine included getting up every morning at 3:00 a.m. for prayer, followed by a search of the skies at 4:00 a.m. for some tangible evidence of a spacecraft. Concluding that a spaceship was lurking behind the Hale-Bopp comet that had made its visible appearance in the northern sky, thirty-nine members of Heaven's Gate quickly became obsessed with departure. Over a three-day period, they systematically killed themselves, each one dying with his or her passsport and a suitcase packed for what each apparently thought was a rendezvous with a UFO trailing the Hale-Bopp comet.

Heaven's Gate is just one of thousands of new religious groups and movements that have spawned in America over the past two centuries. Freedom of religion and the spirit of pluralism and diversity have been some of the key ingredients for new religions to germinate and at times attain mainstream status.

### The History of Cults

The history of the past 2,000 years indicates that new religions often arise and flourish during periods of social unrest, political dissent, and spiritual uncertainty. When people feel that the moral fabric of society is unraveling and that mainstream religions are no longer providing answers to life's big questions, it is then that many seek alternatives to traditional churches or are impelled to create new religions. A prime example of this occurred from the fourteenth to the seventeenth centuries, when all kinds of social, political, and religious movements sprang to life, including the Protestant Reformation.

During the past 175 years, there have been three significant time periods where America experienced a rash of new and exotic religions. The first of these was between 1820 and 1890, a time of rapid social and economic changes, as well as an era of spiritual revivals that were often controversial and divisive. As a result, not only did major splits occur within many denominations, but a large number of new religious groups, generally labeled as sects or cults, sprang up everywhere. The term *sect* generally refers to a protest movement, a group that splinters off from a major denomination in an attempt to restore the true faith. Examples of sects that started during this time were the Millerites, the Unitarians, Holiness churches, and the Seventh-day Adventists.

The most popular label for new religions is the term *cult*. Whereas a sect is usually a spinoff from another religion, a cult is something new, unique, and generally independent of established religion. This category included New Thought or Religious Science (the forerunner of the New Age movement), Mormonism, modern Spiritualism, Mesmerism, Christian Science, and Jehovah's Witnesses.

The early sects and cults opened the floodgates for all kinds of unconventional beliefs and movements to surface. Popping up at every corner were preachers, faith healers, seers, mediums, traveling medicine men, shamans offering magic elixirs, and a wave of idealists advocating all manner of radical ideologies and utopian societies. Two examples of utopian settlements were the Oneida Community of New York and the Amana Society in Iowa. What started out as close-knit communal villages that focused on perfection and separation from the world are today commercial enterprises best known for their production of silverware and kitchen appliances.

The second great wave of new religions in the United States occurred in the 1960s and 1970s. Massive social and political changes—protest marches, the drug culture, the sexual revolution, rampant individualism, revolt against authority, boredom with traditional values, the influence of Eastern spirituality, and the surge of religious experimentation—all of these created a climate for thousands of new religious groups to spring to life. Many of these cults drew heavily on Eastern philosophies in which transcendental meditation, yoga, and various other mind-altering practices were prominent. These two decades popularized such groups as the Hare Krishna, scores of New Age and UFO cults, Scientology, and the Unification Church (the Moonies).

The third wave involved a burst of new cults in the 1980s that focused on mental health, psychotherapy, prosperity groups (sometimes called "commercial" cults), and an explosion of the occult. During the past two or three decades literally millions of people have been lured into one or more of these groups. They may include self-help or encounter groups, business-training workshops, prosperity programs, psychotherapy clinics, martial-arts centers, spiritual-awakening seminars, personal-improvement courses, and campus fellowship groups.

Generally speaking, psychological or prosperity cults are highly persuasive programs, designed to drastically alter people's worldview, their personal philosophy, spiritual beliefs, and work-related practices. The lifestyle, relationships, or beliefs once held by cult members are usually branded by the cult as irrelevant or evil. Through direct solicitation or well-honed recruitment tactics, cults subtly hook people into pay-as-you-go programs, which gradually demand greater and greater commitment, as well as buying more and more expensive courses. Too often the full story and the real purpose of the cult—to manipulate and control people so as to induce dependence on the group—is not discovered until members are deeply enmeshed within the cult. Cults have so professionalized their approaches and techniques that they are rapidly moving from the fringe to the mainstream of society.

Since the word *cult* has become such a negative label, some have replaced it with terms like the *religious fringe*, or *alternative religion*. Generally speaking, there is no consensus as to what defines or constitutes a cult. What may be considered as an "organized heresy" by some may be viewed as quite orthodox by others. There are those whose view of a cult is simply anyone whose religion doesn't agree with their own! Cults can be any size, ranging from a handful of people to millions of members. Cults are associated with virtually all world religions, and what may be viewed as a cult by one religion may not be so recognized by the oth-

ers. From a Christian perspective, cults can be described as religious or commercial groups that appear to be Christian but whose core beliefs and practices are not in harmony with the established teachings of Christianity.

### Characteristics of Cults

Here are some examples of traits and qualities that usually characterize cults:

• **Twisting of biblical truths:** The basic **trademark** of all cults is that Jesus and salvation by grace through faith alone are not central. Cults are works-oriented, and thus their primary focus is cult-sponsored activities.

• **Promoting the leader's authority:** The supreme authority of Scripture is often replaced by authoritarian leadership. Rather than man turning **to** God, it's man turning **into** God. Cults are usually maintained "from the top down."

• **Redefining of biblical terms:** biblical terms are used in ways that harmonize with the way the cult has redefined them rather than in the scriptural meaning. Cults will say one thing publicly but privately mean something totally different.

• **Disregarding sound principles of Bible study:** Cults employ unsound or even bizarre methods of interpretation to support their doctrines. Many cults will simply ignore the Bible and replace it with their own sacred writings or private "revelations."

• **Demanding absolute loyalty:** Cult members have little opportunity for reflection, critical thinking, or freedom of thought and expression. Group loyalty supersedes all other ties and relationships.

- **Employing mind-control techniques:** Fear, guilt, and other social pressures are used to create a sense of powerlessness and to get members to become almost totally dependent on the cult for all major decisions.

- **Utilizing fraud and deception:** Cults have a tendency to misrepresent themselves when fund raising and often do their recruiting and witnessing under false pretenses. It is their belief that the end justifies the means.

- **Consuming dedication and commitment:** Members generally put in extremely long hours of witnessing, distributing literature, and fund raising for the organization. These are generally carried out to the neglect of family and other responsibilities.

- **Growing antagonism to Christian churches:** Cults often flaunt their independence and generally identify themselves in opposition to Christian churches.

- **Experiencing a persecution complex:** Cults tend to stir up an "us vs. them" mentality in order to enhance commitment and unify the group.

- **Demanding conformity of belief and lifestyle:** Cults operate within a control-oriented framework. Conformity to the group replaces individual autonomy. Total dependence upon the group is a high priority.

- **Maintaining an exclusivistic position:** Cults tend to emphasize secret rituals and "inside knowledge." Leaders are often looked up to as God's modern-day messengers and revered as the sole channels of truth.

- **Practicing a controlled environment:** Cults are inclined to maintain tight control on members' lives, placing restrictions on what they can see, read, or believe; where they can go; how they spend their money; and with whom they can associate (or even marry!).

## Why Join a Cult?

If cults have such negative features, why then would anyone become involved with them? A common myth as to why people join cults is that they are obviously gullible, stupid, or have serious personality disorders. The fact is that normal, ordinary people are generally the ones who join cults. Those who have studied the cult phenomena and have counseled former cult members have come to some general conclusions as to why people join cults. Here are some of the most common reasons:

- **Traditional churches are no longer relevant:** Very few cult members were actively involved in the church in which they were raised. Cults are especially attractive to those whose interest and involvement in the church have fizzled out because they see traditional religion as boring and irrelevant to their needs, interests, and concerns.

- **People desire simple, straightforward answers:** Cults endeavor to offer instant, decisive, and clear-cut solutions to life's problems. Young people today are overwhelmed by the insecurity and instability of the job market, the loss of family closeness, the complexity of society, the pressure of mounting personal decisions, and the sheer number of choices they have to make. Feeling lost and alone, they find themselves swept along with a group that presents a righteous certainty and offers a straightforward path to success. Secular cults that are especially popular in the business world are highly pragmatic, providing alluring "self-help" programs that promise immediate and tangible (profitable) returns.

• **The need for affirmation and personal involvement:** Former cult members commonly reveal that they were looking for companionship or the opportunity to do something to benefit themselves and others. Many want to leave a negative, hurting environment for one that is supportive and accepting. When teenagers are encouraged to be adventurous, activists, and independent but lack the decision-making skills or appropriate parental guidance, they may be prime candidates for what cults have to offer. Cults endeavor to give people what is lacking in their lives—acceptance, direction, and a sense of empowerment. Cults pretend to be highly idealistic and with great conviction assure their members that they can help them make a difference in the world.

• **Not recognizing vulnerable moments:** People are especially vulnerable to cultic persuasion when they are depressed over a loss or disappointment, have intense feelings of emptiness, or are not engaged in something meaningful. Vulnerable individuals are those who are lonely, in transition between high school and college, between college and a job, traveling away from home, recently arrived in a new location, recently divorced, fired from a job, or feeling overwhelmed about how things are going.

At such times people are more open to suggestions or invitations without thinking that there might be strings attached.

• **A lack of biblical understanding:** People do not usually join a cult because they have done a thorough study of various religions and have found that a particular cult presents the best theology available. Since people generally join cults because their personal needs aren't being met in traditional churches, they tend to become involved with a cult before they have a clear idea what it's all about. Cult experts believe that one important factor for the cult explosion in the United States is that churches have failed to make biblical understanding a high priority. Many people who join cults are Christians who were unable to distinguish cultic belief from biblical Christianity. People tend to be more interested in "belonging" than in "believing." They travel from church to church, or from one religious group to another, looking for a religion that is custom-made for their individual needs and interests. When the truths of the Bible are no longer the ultimate standard of spirituality, then the door is open, and the welcome mat is out to alternative religions.

## Anchor Text

"Do not love the world or anything in the world. If anyone loves the world, the love of the Father is not in him. For everything in the world—the cravings of sinful man, the lust of his eyes and the boastings of what he has and does—comes not from the Father but from the world. The world and its desires pass away, but the man who does the will of God lives forever" (1 John 2:15-17).

### WRITER ACKNOWLEDGMENT OF RESOURCES

1. Kyle, Richard. *The Religious Fringe: A History of Alternative Religions in America.* Downers Grove, Ill.: InterVarsity Press, 1993.

2. Singer, Margaret Thaler with Janja Lalich. *Cults in Our Midst.* San Francisco, Calif.: Jossey-Bass Publishers, 1995.

## Bible Search

The Bible acknowledges that religious divisions and offshoots are a reality of life. What can we do to avoid being ensnared by disgruntled religious groups that may appear very persuasive and legitimate? This assignment is designed to answer this question by providing some biblical insights and guidelines.

1. According to the Bible, what generally characterizes a deceptive cult?
   A. Matthew 7:15.

# Reaction

## Discussion Questions

1. What do you see as the pros and cons of a sect? What are the positive and negative consequences of a group's breaking away from a parent denomination?

2. Why do you think Eastern religions and philosophies became so popular in the United States during the 1960s and 1970s?

3. What kind of cults do you think might be most attractive to Seventh-day Adventist teenagers? Explain your answer.

4. In the list of cult characteristics, which five do you think are the most spiritually damaging? Why?

5. Give some examples of "unsound" methods of Bible study.

6. Do you know of anyone who has joined a cult? What do you know about his or her experience as a cult member?

7. What can the Seventh-day Adventist Church do to make religion more relevant to your needs, interests, and concerns?

## Personal Response

People who join cults find their present religious experience boring and irrelevant. What can you do to make your commitment to Jesus Christ alive and meaningful? Have you ever taken the time to consider what the Seventh-day Adventist Church offers you that you would not want to give up in order to join some other religious group?

B. 2 Timothy 4:2-4.

2. How does one determine the merits (the rightness or wrongness) of a religious group?
   A. Matthew 7:16-23.
   B. Isaiah 8:20.

3. What are some identifying characteristics of cult leaders?
   A. Acts 20:29.
   B. Mark 10:42-45.

4. How important is an understanding of the Bible when we are confronted by cults?
   A. Acts 17:11.
   B. Ephesians 4:14, 15.

5. What important guidelines should we follow in our study of the Bible?
   A. 2 Peter 1:20, 21.
   B. 2 Timothy 2:15.
   C. 2 Corinthians 4:2.

6. Of what should we be especially aware as we meet new religious groups?
   2 Corinthians 11:4.

## Practical Application

1. Imagine that you have just read a brief article in a religious magazine that states that the Seventh-day Adventist Church is a cult. The writer defends his view by stating that since Seventh-day Adventists worship on the Sabbath, accept Ellen White as an inspired prophet, and follow Old Testament dietary laws, such beliefs indicate that Seventh-day Adventists are not orthodox and should therefore be considered a "fringe" religion. Write a 300-word response to this article.

2. Though Ellen White did not write very much about cults, she had a great deal to say about mesmerism and hypnotism. Using the *Index to the Writings of Ellen G. White*, look up the references to these terms and read what Ellen White said about them. Write a report of 400 words and share it with the class.

3. Divide into small groups of students and do a presentation on one of the following groups. Your presentation can be done as a skit, a videotape, or a panel discussion.
   A. Unitarians.
   B. Christian Science.
   C. Scientology.
   D. The Unification Church (the Moonies).
   E. A "commercial" cult.
   F. Any cult of recent times, such as Jim Jones and the People's Temple, David Koresh and the Branch Davidians, Heaven's Gate, the reorganization of the World Wide Church of God, etc.

The religion that comes from God is the only religion that can lead to God.

# Lesson 12

## The Casuistry of Cults

In her book *Six Years With God*, Jeanie Mills writes about her time spent with Jim Jones and the People's Temple. She writes, "While we were in it we did many strange things. We signed over all our property. We wrote and signed false, self-incriminating statements. . . . We had to participate in painful punishments for such minor things as forgetting to call Jones 'Father.' . . . We were so frightened of him and his power that we would have sworn to anything he asked. We believed that he would always take care of us and would never harm us, even though we witnessed daily atrocities that should have convinced us otherwise."[1]

Jeanie was raised a Seventh-day Adventist, but following a divorce and remarriage, she no longer felt welcome in her church. In 1969 she, along with her new husband Al and five children, gladly accepted the offer to become members of the People's Temple near Ukiah, California. Their affiliation with this very social and independent church group took them from northern California to Los Angeles and eventually to the jungles of Guyana in South America. At first the family was caught up and blessed by the group's spiritual enthusiasm and extensive outreach programs, but eventually Jones's paranoia and his obsession for power and control led to the strange events she writes about in her book.

Two years after Jeanie, Al, and the three youngest children left the People's Temple in 1976, Jim Jones coerced his followers to drink some punch laced with cyanide, resulting in the death of 912 people, including the Mills' two oldest daughters. But this tragic story didn't end there. About a year after the Mills established the Human Freedom Center in Berkeley, California, to provide counseling for those who had left the People's Temple, Jeanie, Al, and their three young children were brutally murdered. Though cults do not generally have these kinds of horror stories associated with them, they all leave behind, to some degree, a trail of spiritual abuse, deception, and disillusionment.

### Cults of the Nineteenth Century

Some of the older, more established cults, such as the Latter Day Saints (Mormons) and the Jehovah's Witnesses, have been around long enough to have attained a favorable status in society. The respect and acceptance they have achieved is due primarily to the sincere, well-meaning, and highly devoted people who make up the majority of their membership. This fact helps us to realize that the real problem with cults is not the general membership but rather with its belief system and leadership practices. In our evaluation of religious groups, no matter how large or small, it is important to focus on **principles** of belief and conduct rather than the **people** themselves.

### Church of Jesus Christ of Latter Day Saints

This religious group, better known as the Mormons, is the wealthiest and one of the most successful alternative religions in American history. Their phenomenal growth

> **"Even though we, or an angel from heaven, should preach to you a gospel contrary to that which we have preached to you, let him be accursed" (Galatians 1:8, NASB).**

(nearly ten million members), their missionary zeal and sacrificial giving, along with their emphasis on family togetherness, healthful living, and high moral standards have won for them a positive image. Although the Mormons have some beliefs that are rooted in Christianity, most of their core doctrines are unscriptural, reflecting instead the "new revelations" of their founder Joseph Smith. As a young man, Joseph Smith (1805–1844) spent much time digging for treasure and getting involved in a variety of occult practices, such as the use

of divining rods, seer stones, ritual magic, and astrology. The grand climax to such activity was his claim that the angel Moroni led him in the discovery of the Golden Plates, which, when translated into English, became known as the *Book of Mormon*. The Mormons accept this book as the ultimate Word of God, using it as the standard by which they judge the truthfulness of the Bible. In fact, Joseph Smith described the *Book of Mormon* as "the most correct of any book on the earth, and the keystone of our religion."[2]

Mormons claim that they alone preach "the fullness of the everlasting gospel" that was made known to Joseph Smith by the angel Moroni. But the apostle Paul warns, "Even though we, or an angel from heaven, should preach to you a gospel contrary to that which we have preached to you, let him be accursed" (Galatians 1:8, NASB). An examination of the Mormon gospel reveals that it is indeed **"contrary"** to the biblical gospel.

For example, Mormons teach that (1) it was necessary for Adam to sin in order for humankind to experience joy, happiness, and "external exaltation" (perfection), a step-by-step process attained by obedience to Mormon laws and temple rituals. There is no salvation by grace in Mormon theology. (2) God is not eternal and infinite, but rather, he was born a man, named Elohim, who achieved divinity. Jesus and Lucifer are brothers, Elohim's literal sons. (3) God is a polygamist who mates with female deities to produce an abundance of spirits or souls. These spirits await embodiment in human form; thus Mormons have large families so that human bodies can be provided for as many spirits as possible. With their bodies becoming the habitation of heavenly spirits, Mormonism prohibits the use of alcohol, tobacco, and caffeine. (4) Every faithful Mormon can likewise become a god in the life hereafter, presiding over his or her own world. For Mormons there are many worlds and many gods. (5) Everyone will eventually be saved, but only baptized Mormons will become gods. In order for everyone to be saved, Mormons participate in "proxy" baptism. This involves a three-hour temple ritual during which they are baptized in behalf of someone (dead or alive) who was or is not a Mormon. This unbiblical practice makes spiritualism rampant within Mormonism.[3]

It is evident from just a cursory look at some of the core beliefs and practices of Mormonism why it is generally viewed today as an "alternative" religion rather than a Christian denomination.

**The Jehovah's Witnesses**

There is a difference of opinion today among Christian scholars as to whether Jehovah's Witnesses are a sect or a cult. They do have Christian roots, in that their founder Charles Taze Russell (1852–1916) was greatly influenced by Adventism before he established the Zion's Watchtower Bible and Tract Society in 1884. Even though Jehovah's Witnesses consider themselves to be the only "true Christians," they openly repudiate many of the fundamental beliefs of Christianity and reveal their disdain for traditional religion by referring to their

houses of worship as "Kingdom Halls" rather than churches.

Jehovah's Witnesses are perhaps the most separatist of the older fringe religions. Their unorthodox beliefs and lifestyle make meaningful dialogue and interaction with society virtually impossible. Their radical antiworld attitude will not allow them to salute the flag, stand for the national anthem, vote, hold a government office, serve in the armed forces, join a labor union or any secular organization. On a more personal level, they will not pray with nor tend to develop close relationships with non-Witnesses; totally "shun" former members (even within the family); avoid celebrating birthdays, Christmas, and Easter holidays; and generally stay away from institutions of higher learning. One taboo that has led to many lawsuits and much unfavorable publicity is their resistance to blood transfusions. This belief is based on a very literal interpretation of the biblical command not to eat any flesh that contains blood. (See Leviticus 3:17; Acts 15:20, 29.)

Jehovah's Witnesses reject the doctrine of the Trinity, believing it to be unbiblical. Like the ancient Arians or modern Unitarians, they believe that Christ is a created being and that the Holy Spirit is simply the invisible life force of God. In 1961 they published the *New World Translation of the Holy Scriptures*, a highly biased translation that is used exclusively by Jehovah's Witnesses to justify their peculiar doctrines.

Like the Mormons, they teach that salvation is not received as a free gift but by obedience to the commands of God. On the other hand, Jehovah's Witnesses agree with the Seventh-day Adventists that the soul of man is not immortal and that at the end of time the wicked are totally destroyed and do not suffer eternal torment in hell.

Jehovah's Witnesses maintain that the Second Coming has already occurred in three stages—invisible appearances of Christ in 1874, 1914, and 1918. Believing that Christ's kingdom has already been established on earth, Jehovah's Witnesses are now awaiting the Battle of Armageddon. Early on, they predicted that this would occur in 1925. In 1966, the leadership once again made a bold prediction: Armageddon and the end of the world would take place in 1978. When the year passed and nothing happened, about 30,000 Witnesses gave up their faith.

Jehovah's Witnesses regard every member as an ordained minister and an active missionary. Besides attending five regular meetings each week in the Kingdom Hall, the average member is expected to spend at least ten hours per month in door-to-door witnessing and giving away *The Watchtower* and *Awake* magazines. Some Witnesses, referred to as special pioneers, may spend as much as ninety or more hours a month in witnessing, giving Bible studies, and selling literature.

Believing that all other religions are false, Witnesses are forbidden to read any literature, in Kingdom Halls or in their homes, that is not published by their own organization. The position by the Jehovah's Witnesses' hierarchy that their organization, their translation of the Bible, their doctrines, and their literature are the only expressions of true religion in the world is being increasingly challenged by its members. Influenced by spiritual diversity and freedom of thought in today's society, and embarrassed repeatedly by failed predictions, published retractions, reinterpretations, and apologies by their authoritarian governing board, there is increased restlessness and a clamor for change that is bound to take place in the years ahead.

## Cults of the Twentieth Century

Twentieth-century cults are those that sprang into existence or were popularized in the past three or four decades and are markedly different from the older, more established ones. Many of the newer cults tend to be more world-affirming and try to appear less overtly Christian or religious. They represent an alternative spirituality that is generally characterized by Eastern philosophies, tend to focus on everyday issues rather than doctrines or morality, and allow members to participate without ever setting foot inside a church. There are literally hundreds of groups that fit that description, with most of them coming under the umbrella of the New Age movement.

## The New Age Movement

The New Age movement is a large, loosely structured network of coalitions, organizations, and individuals all striving to induce a new age of enlightenment and harmony in the world. Although some trace its origin to the cultural revolution of the 1960s, **New** Age is basically a new, appealing form of a very **old** error—ancient ideas expressed with a modern vocabulary. At the heart of New Age thinking is the denial of an infinite God who is distinct from creation. It sees humankind's basic problem as ignorance of its unlimited potential—it's own divinity. It maintains that the human race mistakenly sees itself separated from God as a result of its presently limited consciousness. Thus the New Age advances the idea that humankind must leave the Piscean Age—an age represented by the sign of the fish (a symbol of Christianity), and enter the Aquarian Age—an age of harmony, worldwide oneness, and a higher (godlike) consciousness. It is the goal of the New Age to promote a new worldview and provide the tools and the techniques by which this global reshaping of humankind can take place.

The spiritual philosophy of the New Age is the key to the morals it embraces and the methods it uses to attain its objectives. Because the New Age has its roots in pantheism, God is viewed as an impersonal life

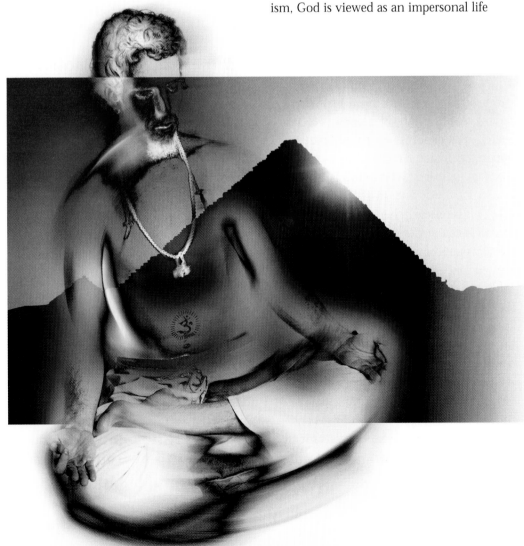

force, a universal energy, a divine consciousness that is the basic essence of all things. In such a worldview, everything and everyone is God. New Agers explain that people do not generally sense their inner divinity because they are victims of a false sense of separation from God. Failure to discern the "divine within"—the Higher Self, can be resolved only by a "consciousness revolution"—experiencing personal transformation that is attained through New Age technology. New Age offers a wide array of psychospiritual techniques that are geared to dispel antiquated ideas of human weakness and depravity and to ignite people's infinite energies and unleash their divine capabilities.

The awful truth is that when a person becomes his or her own "god," loving and serving oneself will be life's primary focus. Such a spiritual viewpoint opens up the door to an endless array of soul-destroying ideas and practices. When the reality of a transcendent God and divinely revealed absolutes is rejected, then rightness and wrongness are up for grabs. Without objective standards of truth, there are no ultimate answers, only the ebb and flow of the Tao, the cycles of the Yin and Yang, the light and shadowy sides of The Force.

New Age influences virtually every area of life: medicine, science, business, the workplace, the classroom, psychology, ecology, religion, government, sports, music, television, and movies. The New Age way of thinking and doing is often endorsed and implemented through various motivational training seminars, alternative (holistic)

health care, yoga, transcendental meditation, visualization and guided imagery, self-hypnosis and past-lives therapy, channeling, spirit guides, crystal power, chanting, reincarnation, and astrology.

These impressive and alluring New Age concepts are all highly publicized and promoted from a non-Christian perspective. It is imperative, therefore, that our evaluation be firmly grounded on biblical principles. On what basis can certain kinds of motivational seminars, holistic health practices, yoga, meditation, or visualization be acceptable? Why are some kinds unacceptable? Ask yourself the following questions. A negative response indicates that whatever you are confronted with is New Age and contrary to Scripture.

• Does it clearly point to Jesus Christ as your Savior and Lord, the only way to God and eternal life?

• Does it reject the concept that God is an impersonal life-force that can be manipulated through human techniques?

• Does it affirm that the ultimate solutions to life's problems are found in God and in His Word rather than within ourselves?

• Does it reject the concept that man is innately immortal and that we can communicate with the deceased?

In the years ahead, New Age fads and fancies will come and go, but its underlying philosophy will continue to resurface in new forms and practices until the very end of time. There are times when non-Christian religions and Eastern philosophies profitably share their ancient wisdom with the world, providing us with some practical insights into healthful living, igniting new awareness in caring for the environment, or promoting harmony and peaceful ways in resolving human conflicts. But when it comes to life's paramount issues—the truth about God, sin, and eternal life—the wisdom of earthly religions and human philosophies is all foolishness. New Age foolhardedly promises people that they are their own savior. Christianity affirms that Jesus Christ is our wisdom, our righteousness, our salvation. Jesus Himself declared that only as we accept God's grace as it is in Him can we truly "have life—life in all its fullness" (John 10:10, TEV).

## Anchor Text

"What this world considers to be wisdom is nonsense in God's sight. As the scripture says, 'God traps the wise in their cleverness'; and another scripture says, 'The Lord knows that the thoughts of the wise are worthless.' No one, then, should boast about what men can do" (1 Corinthians 3:19-21, TEV).

### NOTES

1. Jeanie Mills, *Six Years With God* (New York, N.Y.: A & W Publishers, Inc., 1979), front and back jacket flaps.

2. Joseph Smith, Jr., *The Book of Mormon* (Salt Lake City, Utah: The Church of Jesus Christ of Latter-day Saints, 1990), Introduction.

3. Affirmed by Ed Decker in the video "Joseph Smith's Temple of Doom." Decker was a former Mormon elder for nineteen years and is co-editor of the book *The God Makers*.

### WRITER ACKNOWLEDGMENT OF RESOURCES

Braswell, George W. Jr. *Understanding Sectarian Groups in America*. Nashville, Tenn.: Broadman Press, 1986.

Winker, Eldon K. *The New Age Is Lying to You*. St. Louis, Mo.: Concordia Publishing House, 1994.

## Bible Search

Since New Age philosophy and thinking has saturated society, no doubt you will be confronted by enticing offers and severe tests in the future. How will you respond? Will you be able to defend the choice you are going to make? In this assignment you are to prepare a six-minute presentation explaining why you, as a Seventh-day Adventist, reject New Age concepts or practices.

A. In preparation for writing your presentation, read the following texts and briefly explain the bearing each has on the New Age.

B. From this list of texts, choose the ones you wish to use and incorporate them into your presentation.

Genesis 11:1-9
Deuteronomy 18:9-14
Isaiah 8:19, 20
Isaiah 14:12-14
Matthew 24:24
Mark 7:21-23
Colossians 1:16, 17
1 Thessalonians 4:16-18
1 John 5:11, 12.

# Reaction

## Discussion Questions

1. How important is it for a religious organization to have a positive image?

2. What do you see as the most serious error of Mormonism?

3. How would your approach differ when sharing your faith with a Jehovah's Witness or witnessing to a Mormon?

4. What do you see as the most alluring feature of the New Age movement?

5. What is the primary reason for maintaining good health?

6. Do you think the Bible supports the Jehovah's Witnesses' refusal to have blood transfusions? Explain your answer.

7. Several guidelines are given in the lesson that should be followed when dealing with the New Age. Can you think of any other biblical guidelines?

## Personal Response

You may be involved at the present with a New Age practice that you have thought was a harmless activity or perhaps a very useful one. Are you willing to evaluate this practice in light of what the Bible teaches and ask God to help you make the right decision?

## Practical Application

1. For nearly two decades, Dr. John Harvey Kellogg boldly promoted the idea of "God in nature" within the Seventh-day Adventist Church. In his book *The Living Temple*, published in 1903, Kellogg wrote, "What is nature?—Nature is simply a philosophical name for God, who is the active force in nature—the 'all in all' " (page 6). In combating this error, Ellen White was inspired of God to point out the dangers of pantheism; this warning is preserved in what is known today as *Testimonies for the Church*, volume 8. Read pages 255-266 and 290-294. You can choose either to write a 300-word summary of your reading or write 15 statements that you find the most interesting and helpful.

2. Divide into groups of two or three and do a class presentation on one of the following groups. Your presentation could involve a skit, a panel discussion, or an oral presentation.
   A. Mormons.
   B. Jehovah's Witnesses.
   C. A New Age practice.

3. Attend a Mormon, Jehovah's Witnesses, or a Christian Science church service and interview one or more members. If this is not feasible, do a personal interview with a member of one of these groups. Prepare to give an oral presentation of your 350-word report.

Truth is eternal, knowledge is changeable. It is disastrous to confuse them.

# Lesson 13

## The Darkness of This World

Sean Sellers has occupied a prison cell in the state penitentiary in McAlester, Oklahoma, for over ten years. At the age of seventeen, Sean became the youngest inmate on death row awaiting the execution of the death penalty by lethal injection.

Sean was born to Vonda and Jason Sellers while they were both teenagers. Shortly after Sean's birth, their marriage ended in divorce. About three years later, Vonda married Lee, a cross-country truck driver with whom she had been living for a couple of years. While Vonda and Lee were on the road, Sean was generally taken care of by his grandparents, baby sitters, or friends and neighbors. With little supervision and guidance over the next ten to twelve years, Sean was usually free to make his own choices as to what music he listened to, what movies he watched, what activities he became involved in, or the kids he hung around with. An agenda like that is bound to lead to disaster!

Natural naiveté, the desire for fun and adventure, and a growing resentment for not having a better relationship with his parents eventually led him into the world of the occult. It all started innocently enough—with fun and games. As Sean looks back, he believes that what really turned his life downward was playing Dungeons and Dragons and being introduced to witchcraft by one of the persons who took care of him. By the time Sean started high school, he was deeply involved in Satanism. Believing that committing murder was a Satanic obligation, Sean and a close friend chose to kill a convenience-store clerk. But this only fueled the flames of emptiness and rebellion that were in Sean's heart. And so late one night after coming home from the pizza place where he worked, Sean took his stepfather's shotgun and murdered him and Sean's mother as they lay sleeping in bed. And so today Sean sits on death row! In reality, anyone involved with the dark forces of this world is sitting on death row.

### The Reality of the Occult

There are two ways to be fooled: One is to believe what isn't so; the other is to refuse to believe what is so. This is especially true when it comes to the supernatural realm. When dealing with the occult, people tend toward either of two extremes: Dismiss as nonsense the whole idea of the occult or else have an excessive interest in the subject. We need to avoid either extreme.

The Bible makes it clear that we live in a world that is infiltrated and influenced by powerful demons. When Satan tempted Adam and Eve, it was only the beginning of a cleverly devised plan to deceive and control all of humankind. Satan's strategy was to involve this planet in his ultimate ambition to overthrow the highest administration in the universe—God's government. Such an act of treason is clearly revealed in Lucifer's original battle cry: "I will exalt my throne above the stars of God. . . . I will be like the most High" (Isaiah 14:13, 14, KJV). This clamor for ultimate **power** and **control** is an obsession that is shared alike by Satan and fallen humankind. The underlying purpose of angelic or human rebellion is exactly the same: Dethrone God and let Self rule.

Paul warns us of an ongoing controversy between the forces of good and evil with these words: "We are not fighting against human beings but against the wicked spiritual forces in the heavenly world, the rulers, authorities, and cosmic powers of this dark age" (Ephesians 6:12, TEV). Scripture makes it clear that Egypt had its magicians and enchanters, Babylon relied on astrologers and wise men, Rome highly esteemed its mediums and heathen deities, and even the Jewish nation during much of the Old Testament and at the time of Jesus was rampant with demonic activity. In Revelation, John describes the worldwide magnitude of this warfare when he states that "Babylon"—a symbol of the corrupt **religious** systems of the world "has become a home for demons and a haunt for every evil spirit" (Revelation 18:2). The occult craze of our day has literally captivated the world's attention with its psychic hotlines, angel appearances, occult spectacles, and spiritistic healings.

## The Lure of the Occult

Occultism is a common characteristic of many cults and almost all nontheistic religions. The word *occult* means "hidden" or "secret," having reference to that which is hidden from ordinary perception. Occultism is the attempt to unveil the future or to experience forbidden powers and pleasures that are beyond the range of normal reality. Contacting the supernatural realm to acquire power for personal gratification or to manipulate people or events is extremely dangerous and forbidden by God. Occultism is all about shrugging off moral restraints and catering to the whims and wishes of the carnal nature—an intense form of idolatry.

In today's increasingly pagan culture, great masses of people seem to be insatiably captivated by anything that suggests the mystical, the miraculous, or the angelic. A basic reason for the overwhelming fascination with the occult is that life cannot be lived in a spiritual vacuum. When individuals, societies, or religions **turn away** from the **truths** of the Bible, they will inevitably **turn to** the **lies** and deceptions of the enemy of God. As people lose faith in the saving truths of **divine** revelation, they look for answers, certainty, and reassurance from the **demonic** realm. Driven by an intense desire to find help in untraditional ways or places, people are generally inclined not to test "the spirits to see whether they are from God" (1 John 4:1). This can be as deadly as eating or drinking anything without first checking the list of ingredients. There are, of course, other reasons for not exercising spiritual discernment. First, atheists and humanists do not believe in the supernatural; thus they simply dismiss the demonic realm as an illusion. For them, all occult phenomena, such as séances, astrology, or Ouija board messages, have natural explanations. In the world of high-tech, occultism has exchanged a sinister look for scientific credibility. Second, most Christian churches and cults believe in the natural immortality of the soul, and this makes contacting or communicating with the dead, to a lesser or greater degree, a viable option. Third, religions that view God as a divine energy that can be tapped through prescribed rituals are invariably enmeshed in the occult. The Eastern concept that all reality is divine not only leads to the worship of nature, it also endorses the dangerous idea that the supernatural realm is entirely good. Thus you have the very popular **but mistaken view** that all miraculous sightings or experiences associated with angelic appearances are of heavenly origin. Just because some apparent good has taken place is not sufficient evidence that the event is from God.

**Doorways to the Occult**

The Bible teaches that **all** forms and aspects of the occult are "an *abomination* to the Lord" (Deuteronomy 18:12, NKJV). One definition of abomination is something viewed with "extreme disgust and hatred." There are many kinds of human experiences that serve as a means of contact with the paranormal, the occult, and the demonic. Objects, rituals, or practices that function as doorways or catalysts to the supernatural have been identified for us in God's Word as

Satan's devices. There is a real temptation, however, to think that we are intelligent enough to recognize Satan's devices on our own. But doorways to the occult are cunningly deceptive, having a mysterious and curiously fascinating aura about them. They are so cleverly disguised that initially they give the impression of being positive experiences. They might appear as nothing more than harmless activities or just fun and games. What else would we expect from the greatest deceiver in the universe? We have been duly warned: "There is nothing that the great deceiver fears so much as that we should become acquainted with his devices."[1]

Concepts or practices that are not in harmony with the biblical worldview are to be rejected as spiritually unsafe for the Christian. It is essential that both the immediate effects and the long-range objectives be carefully evaluated in light of the gospel and the overall teachings of God's Word. This point is well illustrated by Eve, whose initial experience at the forbidden tree seemed so positive, her first bite so exceedingly delicious, yet the eventual outcome so spiritually devastating—just as God said it would be.

Paul counsels us: "I tell you, then, do not let anyone deceive you with false arguments, no matter how good they seem to be. . . . Since you have accepted Christ Jesus as Lord, live in union with him. Keep your roots deep in him, build your lives on him, and become stronger in your faith. . . . See to it, then, that no one enslaves you by means of the worthless deceit of human wisdom, which comes from the teachings handed down by men and from the ruling spirits of the universe, and not from Christ" (Colossians 2:4-8, TEV).

### Involvement in the Occult

According to the Bible, the following activities come under the classification of "an abomination to the Lord": astrology, casting spells, enchantments, divination, mediums, necromancy, sorcery, spiritism, witchcraft, and rituals where blood is shed and children are sacrificed. Let's define some of these terms:

• **Astrology:** The belief that the position of the planets and other heavenly bodies at the time of one's birth not only influences but determines one's fortunes, personality, and ultimate destiny. God's condemnation not only includes professional astrologers who gain access to information through occult powers but also the supposedly innocent reading of horoscope columns in newspapers and magazines.

• **Divination:** To foretell the future or perceive hidden knowledge through psychic power. This can involve the use of such popular objects as tarot cards and the crystal ball.

• **Enchantments:** To use occult powers to manipulate people or events with an evil intent. This general term can apply to the casting of spells, fortune telling, calling up evil spirits, sorcery, and the practice of magick. (Whereas *magic* generally refers to sleight of hand, *magick* is becoming a common designation for the use of occult powers.)

• **Satanism:** Although this word is not found in Scripture, it has reference to either the worship of man's carnal nature, the forces or energies of nature, or Satan himself. Worship is generally characterized by secrecy, the clamor for power, self-indulgence, and the deliberate sacrilege of Christian beliefs and practices. Hard-core devil worship can become deadly and violent, including the ritualistic killing of animals and children.[2]

• **Spiritualism:** It is the belief that man is innately immortal, that spirits (or angels) are deceased persons, and that the living can communicate with these spirits (necromancy).

• **Witchcraft:** Modern witchcraft, often known as Wicca, is a revival of ancient paganism. Witches worship nature deities and goddesses; generally practice divination, incantations, and magical spells; and claim the power to communicate with the spirit world.

Having briefly examined some of the things that are "an abomination to the Lord," it's very possible that we may think that good, intelligent people like ourselves would never be enticed by these gross and hideous practices. It is a serious mistake, however, to assume that any of Satan's devices can truly be recognized for what they are—evil and death robed in garments of light (2 Corinthians 11:14, 15). This, too, was demonstrated by Eve's experience in the garden. There was no possible way that Eve's five senses could have alerted her to the fact that one particular tree in Eden could bring only misery and death. That fact was known only because God told her so. The apostle Paul says, "I am afraid that just as Eve was deceived by the serpent's cunning" (2 Corinthians 11:3), so people today continue to look at things where the serpent secretly lurks and find them "pleasing to the eye, and also desirable for gaining wisdom" (Genesis 3:6). Satan is not stupid! What worked for him in Eden still works today. The occult still appeals to the eyes, scintillates the senses, and stimulates the desire for knowledge that is forbidden and unknown.

**The Christian Response to the Occult**

In Ephesians 6, Paul writes about "our struggle . . . against the powers of this dark world." He declares, "Be strong in the Lord and in his mighty power. Put on the full armor of God so that you can take your stand against the devil's schemes." And what is this spiritual "armor" that assures victory against all the allurements and attacks of the demonic realm? Paul responds: "Stand firm then, with the belt of **truth** buckled around your waist, with the breastplate of **righteousness** in place, and with your feet fitted with . . . the **gospel** of peace. [And] take up the shield of **faith**, with which you can extinguish all the flaming arrows of the evil one. Take the helmet of **salvation** and the sword of the **Spirit**, which is the **word of God**. And **pray** in the Spirit on all occasions" (verses 10-18, emphasis added).

As a soldier would be foolish to go into battle with some of the armor missing, the same rules apply in Christian warfare. Every aspect of our lives, all the avenues to the soul must be safeguarded and protected at all times. When we experiment, dabble in, or play around with the occult, we are, in effect, opening the doors of our lives to the enemy, who enters only "to steal and kill and destroy" (John 10:10).

Based on Paul's admonition, here are some simple ground rules that will bring you victory in your warfare against the demonic realm:

• **Claim Christ's victory over the powers of darkness for yourself.** Through the power that Christ provides, you, too, can overcome the temptations of the enemy (Revelation 12:11). In Christ's righteousness we stand **perfect** before God, and in Christ's blood we stand **protected** from the enemy. "Greater is He who is in you than he that is in the world" (1 John 4:4, NASB).

• **Dedicate yourself fully to Jesus each day in prayer.** Openly acknowledge that your security and deliverance is possible only through an abiding faith relationship with Christ. Be very specific in your requests, asking God for His help in those areas where you are weak and vulnerable. "Submit yourselves, then, to God. Resist the devil, and he will flee from you" (James 4:7).

• **Immerse yourself in the Word of God.** What we need in dealing with the alluring power of occult ideas and practices is a knowledge that is firmly grounded in God's Word and made powerfully effective by the indwelling of His Spirit. When you obey its precepts and heed its warnings, the Bible enables you to discern and overcome what is evil, which otherwise might appear good and acceptable. "I have hidden your word in my heart that I might not sin against you" (Psalm 119:11).

• **Separate yourself from all occult objects and materials.** Refrain from watching, reading, or participating in any form of occult practice or activity. This includes such things as role playing games, music, or movies that feature violence, horror, and occult themes. David's prayer, "I will set nothing wicked before my eyes" (Psalm 101:3, NKJV), must be a guiding principle of our lives as well. With God's help, focus on that which stimulates purity, strengthens your spiritual nature, and brings honor and glory to Jesus.

## Anchor Text

"Though we live in the world, we do not wage war as the world does. The weapons we fight with are not the weapons of the world. On the contrary, they have divine power to demolish strongholds. We demolish arguments and every pretension that sets itself up against the knowledge of God, and we take captive every thought to make it obedient to Christ" (2 Corinthians 10:3-5).

# Reaction

## Discussion Questions

1. Why do you think the Old Testament has much less to say about Satan than does the New Testament?

2. What do you think you should do if you discover that a friend of yours is deeply involved in the occult?

3. When you hear of an angelic rescue or intervention where a life has been spared, is it safe to assume that it was of a heavenly origin? Explain your answer.

4. Your lesson states that any practice that is not in harmony with the biblical worldview must be rejected by the Christian. Is this always true? Explain your answer.

5. Do you see anything significant about the fact that both Adventism and Spiritualism began around the same time?

6. Do you think Satan can read a person's mind? Foretell the future?

## Personal Response

A few years ago a credit-card company popularized the advertising slogan "Don't leave home without it." In a spiritual sense, you and I should not leave home or dorm room without HIM. Are you willing each morning to dedicate your life to God, to grant Him audible permission to protect you from the evil that surrounds you, and to fill your heart and mind with truth and love that can be graciously shared with others throughout the day?

**NOTES**

1. White, Ellen G. *The Great Controversy* (Nampa, Idaho,: Pacific Press, 1950), page 516.

2. Ankerberg, John and John Weldon, *The Coming Darkness* (Eugene, Ore.: Harvest House, 1993).

## Bible Search

1. Use the worksheet "Enemy Tactics" provided by your teacher to do your Bible study on Satan.

2. In heathen religions or modern paganism, idols and occult objects are used to represent the gods or some kind of higher powers. Rituals are used to acknowledge, worship, and submit to these higher powers. For this reason some of the most severe warnings in the Bible are directed against idolatry. Complete the following assignment, using the indicated texts.

   A. Describe the evils associated with idolatry. Deuteronomy 32:16, 17; Psalm 106:34-37; Galatians 5:20; Ephesians 5:5; Colossians 3:5.

   B. Explain why Paul contrasts the sacrifice to idols with participation in the Lord's Supper. 1 Corinthians 10:14-21.

## Practical Application

1. Read the chapter titled "Can Our Dead Speak to Us?" pages 551-562, in the book *The Great Controversy*. As you read the chapter, write ten to fifteen statements that describe either the beliefs, the power, or the effects of spiritualism.

2. Make a collage that illustrates how today's media is a powerful tool for promotion of the occult.

3. Which occult practice do you think some of the students in your school may be involved in because they see it as a harmless activity? Complete either A or B. (A) Prepare a three- to five-minute oral presentation on this activity. You can share a personal experience or that of someone else, or do some research on the topic. (B) Team up with another student and write and present a five-minute skit that illustrates how one person can help another in turning away from an occult practice.

Jesus paid a debt He didn't owe because we had a debt we couldn't pay.

# Lesson 14

## The World's Only Savior

We all enjoy a heart-to-heart talk with our friends. And so did Jesus. But none was as significant as the dialogue He had with His twelve disciples about six months before His death. Shortly before this occasion, He had performed one of His greatest miracles in feeding the 5,000 with a lad's five loaves and two fishes. After this unusual meal, the awestruck disciples, along with the people, decided to "make him king by force" (John 6:15). Why shouldn't they? Wasn't it obvious that He was the right man for the job! For a person with political ambition, such a move on the part of one's admirers would have been welcomed. But for Jesus it was extremely disheartening. Not even the people closest to Him understood the real purpose of His mission as the Messiah. Obviously, He had failed to make it clear to the Twelve that His ultimate goal was dying on the cross rather than ruling on a throne. And so Jesus took a break from His public ministry and led His disciples to a quiet, isolated place where He could talk openly and directly with them.

"When Jesus came to the region of Caesarea Philippi, he asked his disciples, 'Who do people say the Son of Man is?' They replied, 'Some say John the Baptist; others say Elijah; and still others, Jeremiah or one of the prophets.' 'But what about you?' he asked. 'Who do you say I am?' Simon Peter answered, 'You are the Christ, the Son of the living God.' Jesus replied, 'Blessed are you, Simon son of Jonah, for this was not revealed to you by man, but by my Father in heaven.'

"From that time on Jesus began to explain to his disciples that he must go to Jerusalem and suffer many things at the hands of the elders, chief priests and teachers of the law, and that he must be killed and on the third day be raised to life. Peter took him aside and began to rebuke him, 'Never, Lord!' he said. 'This shall never happen to you!' Jesus turned and said to Peter, 'Get behind me, Satan! You are a stumbling block to me; you do not have in mind the things of God, but the things of men'" (Matthew 16:13-17, 21-23).

Jesus had numerous private conversations with people—Nicodemus, the Samaritan woman, the rich young ruler, the woman caught in adultery, Zacchaeus, Mary and Martha, Pilate, the thief on the cross—to name just a few. Every one of them had his or her share of really serious problems. But in none of these situations did Jesus respond as severely and as decisively as He did with Peter.

### The Centrality of the Cross

What did Peter say that was so terribly wrong? Simply put, Peter's statement was a denial of everything Christianity stands for. The death and resurrection of Jesus is neither unnecessary nor optional; it is the very heart and soul of Christianity. Jesus knew that His death had been decreed from eternity, for He was "the Lamb slain from the foundation of the world" (Revelation 13:8, NKJV). And when John the revelator was given a glimpse into heaven itself, the ascended Christ appears as a "Lamb looking as if it had been slain" (Revelation 5:6). The scars of the cross are etched into eternity. While the cross represents humankind's only hope of salvation, it also reveals God's

## The scars of the cross are etched into eternity.

holiness and love. Consistent with His holiness, He justly enforces the death penalty for the sinner's transgression. In harmony with His love for us, God, in the person of Jesus Christ, substitutes Himself in the sinner's behalf. This is the **underlying theme** of all Scripture. Paul endorses this point when he declares that the only thing he needed to know was "Jesus Christ and him crucified" (1 Corinthians 2:2). It is at the cross where human evil is exposed, our pride is broken, reconciliation is received, our sin is forgiven, our love rekindled, our hopes restored, and our lives transformed. Without a crucified and risen Savior, the claims of Christianity are empty and

devoid of meaning. As Paul says, "If Christ has not been raised, your faith is futile; you are still in your sins" (1 Corinthians 15:17).

### Religions Without a Cross

Imagine the scene shifting from an isolated hillside of the past to a plush convention center of the present. In this meeting where the representatives of all the world's religions are gathered, Jesus once again asks the question: "Who do you say that I am?" After a lengthy period of silence, a gentleman arises to speak: "We Hindus believe that God is All, and All is God. To us Brahman is the Universal Consciousness, and the many gods that we worship are simply manifestations of the Divine One. The gods that appear in human form on earth are avatars, and we are thankful to you, Jesus, like Krishna, Kali, and Rama, for coming to this earth many times during your incarnations."

Another man quickly stands to his feet: "When we Muslims recite the Shahada, we declare that there is 'no God but Allah.' We believe that there have been many prophets, such as Adam, Noah, Abraham, David, Jonah, Jesus, and, of course, Mohammed, who is the last and greatest of Allah's messengers. I do not mean to be disrespectful to you, Jesus, but Muslims do not accept the Bible's claim that you are God or the Son of God. According to Islamic teachings, Allah would never allow an honored prophet to be crucified, and so at His command, you ascended to heaven and it was Judas who died."

Next to speak is a young lady: "As a Taoist I don't think your question is relevant. What I may believe about you as an honored man of the past has no significance in today's world. The only way the world will ever experience oneness and peace is when we learn to get in touch with the natural flow of the Tao. The secret to life is not found in trusting in a Messiah or worshiping a particular god, but rather, it's living in harmony with the eternal principles of the Yin and Yang.

Before she has finished speaking, an elderly man has already stepped to another microphone. "Judaism believes the Hebrew Scriptures when it declares, 'The Lord our God is one Lord' (Deuteronomy 6:4, KJV). God is not a divided Deity. Our belief in the God of heaven means that we could never accept you as God on earth. Your claim to be the long-awaited Messiah is without scriptural foundation, and so we Jews continue to look for a Messianic age that will restore to the Jews their honor and dignity and usher in universal peace and brotherhood."

As he concludes, there is already a long line of people waiting their turn to speak. There's a Buddhist, a Confucianist, a Zoroastrian, a Shintoist, a Sikh, a Neo-pagan, a Jain, a Shaman, a Native American, a New Ager, as well as representatives from a wide assortment of smaller religious groups and cults. Though great diversity in belief and practice are expressed, there is a common consensus: Salvation is dependent on the **efforts and devotion of humankind** rather than on the **life and death of a Messiah**. And Christ's response is the same as it was to Peter nearly 2,000 years ago: All of "you are a stumbling block to me; you do not have in mind the things of God, but the things of men."

## Contrasting the True and the False

In this unit we have explored major worldviews, the great religions, Christian denominations, various cults, and the occult. But as was stated in a previous lesson, the Bible knows only two religions: the religion of God and the religion of humankind. The conflict that these opposing forms of worship have generated is repeatedly demonstrated from Genesis 3 to Revelation 22. Let us take a look at a compelling illustration of these contrasting principles.

In Genesis 11 we read, "Now the whole world had one language and a common speech. . . . Then they said, 'Come, let us build ourselves a city, with a tower that reaches to the heavens, so that we may make a name for ourselves and not be scattered over the face of the whole earth'" (verses 1-4). The most energetic building project the world had ever seen up to that time was a spiritual quest for "the heavens." The builders had agreed that the Tower of Babel (interpreted by the Babylonians as the "gateway of the gods") should be built in order to provide for their safety in case of another flood. Not only would the work of their own hands bring them the security they sought, the magnificence and splendor of their achievement would capture the admiration of the world, as well as demonstrate their self-sufficiency.

These self-serving aspirations came about because the people refused to rely on God's promises of salvation, rejected His commands to scatter over the entire earth, and rebelled against His divine rulership. The Tower of Babel, which became Babylon, clearly illustrates the primary characteristic of false religion—our attempt to **ascend** to the heavens by our own efforts. Did not Lucifer himself declare, "I will ascend into heaven. I will exalt my throne"? (Isaiah 14:13, NKJV). As Lucifer's self-serving ambition resulted in his downfall, so spirituality based on human endeavors is also doomed to fail. With a "mighty voice" God warns the world that human religions cannot save, declaring, "Babylon the great is fallen, is fallen, and has become a habitation of demons. . . . Come out of her, my people, lest you share in her sins, and lest you receive of her plagues" (Revelation 18:2-4, NKVJ).

The grandiose schemes of Babel's builders stand in stark contrast to the simple story of Jacob's dream. "So [Jacob] came to a certain place and stayed there all night, because the sun had set. . . . Then he dreamed, and behold, a ladder was set up on the earth, and its top reached to heaven; and there the angels of God were ascending and descending on it. . . . And behold, the Lord stood above it and said: . . . 'I am with you and will keep you wherever you go . . . ; I will not leave you until I have done what I have spoken to you.' Then Jacob awoke from his sleep and said, 'Surely the Lord is in this place, and I did not know it.' And he was afraid and said, 'How awesome is this place! This is none other than the house of God, and this is the gate of heaven!' " (Genesis 28:11-17, NKJV).

Human religion builds stairways from earth to heaven for us to **ascend** to where God is. True religion is a ladder let down from heaven to earth for God to **descend** to where we are. Humankind's religion claims that there are **numerous ways** we can connect with God; in true religion Jesus Himself is **the way** to God. Alluding to Jacob's ladder, Jesus declared to Nathaniel, "I tell you the truth, you shall see heaven open, and the angels of God ascending and descending on the Son of Man" (John 1:51). Jesus reemphasizes this point when He says, "I am the gate; whoever enters through me will be saved. . . . I have come that they may have life, and have it to the full" (John 10:9, 10). The religions of the world tend to promote human excellence and greatness. They often encourage high moral standards, humanitarian service, and pious devotion. That is all well and good. But without Jesus Christ, there can be no reconciliation with God, no salvation from sin, no holiness of heart, and no hope of eternal life. Those gifts are received freely, and exclusively, through Jesus Christ.

## Anchor Text

"Being found in appearance as a man, he [Jesus] humbled himself and became obedient to death—even death on a cross! Therefore God exalted him to the highest place and gave him the name that is above every name, that at the name of Jesus every knee should bow, in heaven and on earth and under the earth, and every tongue confess that Jesus Christ is Lord" (Philippians 2:8-11).

## Bible Search

The Anchor Text is one of the most profound statements in all of Scripture. Study this passage, along with the others given below, and answer the following questions:

A. What is the reason for Christ's exaltation to the highest place and being given a name above every name? See also Acts 4:12; Revelation 5:12.

B. Summarize what each of these texts says about confessing that Jesus Christ is Lord: Romans 10:9; 1 Corinthians 12:3.

# Reaction

## Discussion Questions

1. Why do non-Christians find it so difficult to recognize their need of a divine Savior or Mediator?

2. When sharing our faith with others, are we as Seventh-day Adventists guilty of talking more about our accomplishments than about the Cross of Christ?

3. What are the different ways the Bible illustrates the fundamental difference between true and false religion?

4. Why did Jesus talk about His death on the cross before He explained to the disciples the need for taking up their own crosses and following Him?

## Personal Response

When others ask you who Jesus Christ is, can you support your answer with Scripture? Does your answer reflect what you truly believe and have experienced, or do you just say things that sound good and mean very little to you? How do you think Jesus would respond to your answer?

## Practical Application

1. Many people say that even though they do not acknowledge Jesus Christ as the Son of God, they do believe that He was a good man and a great teacher. Write a paper explaining why such a position is untenable.

2. Jesus posed the question "Who do you say I am?" to Peter. If Jesus were to ask the same question to the following groups, how do you think they would answer? In small groups discuss how you think they might respond and be prepared to share your conclusions with the class.
   A. Mormons
   B. Jehovah's Witnesses
   C. New Agers
   D. Roman Catholics
   E. Native Americans

# UNIT GLOSSARY

This glossary includes only terms that are not defined or explained in the lessons and may be relatively unfamiliar to the students.

**Arianism:** The belief that Christ is a created being, therefore denying the doctrine of the Trinity.

**Atonement:** The work of God in Christianity by which He restores the broken relationship between Him and sinners through the life, death, and resurrection of Jesus Christ.

**Authoritarian:** The concentration of power in a self-appointed leader or group that demands total submission to its authority.

**Canon:** A rule or standard of judgment; an authoritative list of books accepted as Holy Scripture.

**Confucianism:** A humanistic philosophy/religion that is deeply rooted in Chinese culture. It stresses social order, family structure, as well as ancestor and nature worship.

**Evangelism:** The active presentation of the gospel with the intent of bringing others into a saving relationship with Jesus Christ. (Often used by Adventists to simply mean the effort to bring people into the Adventist Church.)

**Evolution:** The hypothesis that all life forms have, through a natural process, gradually developed from simpler forms.

**Grace:** An act of undeserved kindness. Saving grace is unmerited favor, the sinner receiving the imputed and imparted righteousness of Christ.

**Humanism:** A philiosophy that stresses a human being's essential goodness and that he is "the measure of all things." It regards the cosmos as uncreated, self-existing, and self-sustaining.

**Immaculate Conception:** A Roman Catholic doctrine that affirms that Mary, the mother of Jesus, was preserved immaculate (sinless) from the moment of conception in her mother's womb.

**Individualism:** Allowing individual rights to take precedence over group rights. Individuality becomes individualism when one becomes preoccupied with self-interest.

**Indulgences:** Remission of part or all the punishment that, according to Roman Catholics, is due for sin committed but forgiven.

**Life philosophy:** One's personal conviction as to what life is all about and how it should be lived.

**Liturgy:** A ritual or a group of rites prescribed for public worship.

**Miracle:** An intervention by a supernatural power that transcends but does not violate natural law.

**Mysticism:** A state of mind or a reality beyond reason. Mystics focus on direct communication with God that tends toward occult or visionary experiences.

**New Thought:** A philosophy that arose in the nineteenth century whose primary focus was the infinite potential of every individual and the power of positive thought.

**Paranormal:** That which is supernatural; not scientifically explainable.

**Penance:** Disciplinary measures and self-punishment that Roman Catholicism asks of those who are seeking forgiveness and restoration.

**Shamans:** Spiritual mediums, witch doctors, or medicine men who claim to cure diseases and communicate with the spirit world.

**Shintoism:** The state religion of Japan. It consists of one's devotion to ancestors, nature deities, and the emperor.

**Theosophy:** A belief that arose during the nineteenth century that declared that humankind is always evolving toward divinity through reincarnation. Humankind can save themselves through knowledge gained from many religions and from the spirit world.

**Transcendentalism:** A philosophy that reflects Eastern thought and advocates direct contact between humanity and God. It is a mystical philosophy that emphasizes the spiritual over the material and points a person inward to oneself and to nature as the source of all truth.

**Transcendental Meditation:** An altered state of consciousness that is designed to turn off the mind, enabling one to experience God-consciousness (unity with the divine).

**Transubstantiation:** The Roman Catholic view that the bread and wine are actually changed (in substance) into the body and blood of Christ by the priest during the Eucharist.

**Unitarianism:** A denomination that teaches that God exists as one person, rather than as a Trinity, and that everyone in the end will be saved.

**Zoroastrianism:** A religion of ancient Persia that teaches that the world is engaged in a conflict between the forces of "light" and the spirits of "darkness."

# Acknowledgments and Thanks

Grateful acknowledgment and recognition is given to those who made a valuable contribution to the development of the **Worldviews and Religion** unit of study.

## SECONDARY BIBLE TEXTBOOK STEERING COMMITTEE

The following served on the Secondary Bible Textbook Steering Committee and were responsible for supervising the development of the Student Textbooks, Teacher Editions, and Teacher Resource Manuals for the **Worldviews and Religion** unit of study.

Gerry E. Thompson, Chair, Director of Education, Pacific Union Conference

DeWayne Boyer, Bible Teacher, Takoma Academy

Cherry Lidner Habenicht, Bible Teacher, Wisconsin Academy

Gordon Kainer, Bible Teacher, Loma Linda Academy

Gerald Kovalski, Director of Education, Southern Union Conference

Glenn E. Russell, Bible Teacher, Andrews Academy

## CONSULTANTS AND STAFF

The following provided valuable support services to the Steering Committee during the development of one or more components of the **Worldviews and Religion** unit.

Consultant

Don Weatherall, Assistant Director, North American Division Office of Education

Staff

Shirley Goodridge, editorial assistant and copyright authorizations

Beverly Benson, word processing of manuscripts for Student Textbook and Teacher Edition

Ardyce Weatherall, word processing of manuscripts for Teacher Resource Manual

## WRITER

Gordon Kainer, Bible teacher, Loma Linda Academy served as writer for the **Worldviews and Religion** unit of study. He brought a rich background of experiences as an academy bible teacher and a writing style that adds interest and variety in approaches to the topics covered.

## TEACHERS AND STUDENTS

The teachers and students in the senior academies in the North American Division who field tested from the **Worldviews and Religion** units during the 1996–1997 school years. Their responses on the evaluation questionnaires provided valuable input and insights.

## TEACHER RESOURCE MANUAL WORKSHOP COMMITTEES

Appreciation is extended to those who served on the Teacher Resource Manual Workshop Committee for the **Worldviews and Religion** unit during the summer of 1997. The members were:

Don Weatherall, Chair, Assistant Director, North American Division Office of Education

Jan Fautheree, Bible Teacher, Gem State Academy

Kevin Pride, Bible Teacher, Forest Lake Academy

Ron Torkelsen, Bible Teacher, Pacific Union College Preparatory School

Jan Yakush, Bible Teacher, College View Academy

## PACIFIC PRESS® PUBLISHING ASSOCIATION

Paul Hey, liaison with the Secondary Bible Textbook Steering committee

Bonnie Tyson-Flyn, in-house editor

## DESIGN AND PAGE LAYOUT

GENESIS DESIGN/Matthew Pierce, Bryan Gray

www.genesis-online.com

## PUBLISHERS, AUTHORS, AND AGENTS

Grateful acknowledgment is made to the following publishers, authors, and agents for permission to use and adapt copyrighted materials:

All Scripture references not otherwise credited are from the Holy Bible: New International Version.

Every effort has been made to trace the ownership of all copyrighted material in this book and to obtain permission for its use.

Sincere appreciation is given to the many others who have contributed to the manuscript whose names may not be included.

Pacific Press® Publishing Association for quotations (Lessons 4 and 12) from *Education* and *The Desire of Ages*, by Ellen G. White. Copyright© 1952. Used by permission of Pacific Press® Publishing Association.

Walk Thru the Bible Ministries Inc. for quotation (Lesson 10) from *The Daily Walk*; © Walk Thru the Bible Ministries Inc. All rights reserved. International copyright secured. Used by permission of Walk Thru the Bible. To order call 1-800-877-5539.

Sources for chapter quotes:
Lesson 1—Proverbs 9:10; Lesson 4—see *Education*, 29; Lesson 6—Francis of Assisi; Lesson 9—Robert Segal; Lesson 10—*The Daily Walk*; Lesson 12—*The Desire of Ages*, 189; Lesson 13—Madeleine L'Engel.